PAYING FOR PRESIDENTS

Paying for Presidents

Public Financing in National Elections

Anthony Corrado

1993 ◆ The Twentieth Century Fund Press ◆ New York

The Twentieth Century Fund sponsors and supervises timely analyses of economic policy, foreign affairs, and domestic political issues. Not-for-profit and nonpartisan, the Fund was founded in 1919 and endowed by Edward A. Filene.

Library of Congress Cataloging-in-Publication Data

Corrado, Anthony, 1957–
   Paying for presidents : public financing in national elections /
Anthony Corrado.
       p. cm.
   "A Twentieth Century Fund paper. "
   Includes index.
   ISBN 0-87078-185-5 : $9.95
   1. Campaign funds--United States. 2. Presidents--United States--
Elections.   I. Title.
JK1991.C68   1993
324.7'8'0973--dc20   93–38548
                                                        CIP

Cover design and illustration: Claude Goodwin
Manufactured in the United States of America.
Copyright © 1993 by the Twentieth Century Fund, Inc.

FOREWORD

The interaction of capitalism and free enterprise is given credit for much of the wealth and progress in the United States. But there are areas of human activity where the relentless pursuit of money may not produce salutary results. In our political system, for example, all but the wealthiest who run for office are engaged in almost constant fundraising marathons. The effort intensifies before elections, of course, but in recent years, it has become a routine and substantial component of elected officials' schedules throughout their terms in office. For American politicians, a very large proportion of their direct interactions with citizens involves soliciting, explicitly or by implication, financial support. Sometimes the process is subtle and hard to separate from other regular activities. Often it involves flattery, listening, and small favors, almost courtesies. It can be and is, however, often quite direct and even blunt. Those who contribute have a wide variety of motives, including friendship, ideological communion, the desire for access, and, of course, shadier reasons.

On both sides of the process, the interaction is scarcely ennobling. Nor does it seem to add a great deal of substance to the formulation of public policy. Indeed, one can argue that, in some cases, the effects of fundraising are very negative. Politicians generally hate the process. They also come to view this segment of the public—a group with which they interact constantly—as merely a source of money. The unwelcome task is to please them to the point where they will "cough up." On the other side of the equation, givers easily can conclude that those they support are merely in it for the money or obsessed with the dollars needed for campaigns. The reality, of course, is more complicated and individualistic. But it is a real price we pay in our system.

There have been attempts to remedy the situation, most notably through the introduction of public financing for campaign expenditures. The most visible example of this reform is at the level of presidential campaigns. And while the current system clearly has altered the process in these elections, there is a growing body of criticism of its practical effects. Opponents of public financing are far from giving up on the possibility of rolling back the existing system. And even supporters of the concept have been sharply critical of the loopholes and other shortcomings, which result in massive national fundraising every four years. Whether in reaction to these disappointments, or for other reasons, the terms of the debate have been changed by the public reluctance to continue to participate. The percentage of taxpayers who check off support for presidential campaign funding on their personal income tax forms has declined steadily in recent years. Clearly, it is time for a fresh appraisal of the system.

With this need in mind, the Twentieth Century Fund commissioned Anthony Corrado, assistant professor of government at Colby College and a participant in the management and financing of presidential campaigns as a member of the national staffs of the last three Democratic presidential nominees, to look at the state of presidential campaign finance reform after the experience of the 1992 election. Although he documents considerable weaknesses in the way the process has been operating, he remains convinced of the value of the public financing approach. His work should enrich the current debate in Washington about whether to change or even scrap the existing system.

Corrado's work complements other Fund studies of campaign finance, including Herbert Alexander's paper on the financing of state and local campaigns, *Reform and Reality*; Larry Sabato's paper on campaign finance, *Paying for Elections*; Ross Baker's analysis of legislative PACs, *The New Fat Cats*; Brooks Jackson's *Broken Promise: Why the Federal Election Commission Failed*; as well as a number of studies of electoral issues by Twentieth Century Fund Task Forces, most notably *Voters' Time: Report of the Twentieth Century Fund Commission on Campaign Costs in the Electronic Age; Electing Congress: The Financial Dilemma*; and *What Price PACs?*

On behalf of the Trustees of the Fund, I thank him for his efforts. I believe that they have the potential to sharpen significantly the debate about where the nation should go from here.

Richard C. Leone, *President*
The Twentieth Century Fund
October 1993

CONTENTS

Acknowledgments

T he author wishes to thank Richard C. Leone and Beverly Goldberg of the Twentieth Century Fund, who supported this project from its beginning and whose valuable suggestions and guidance made this paper possible.

This paper also would not have been possible without the dedication and assistance of the staff of the Federal Election Commission's Office of Public Records. Kent Cooper and Michael Dickerson, in particular, expertly guided me through the Commission's reports and ensured that I had access to all necessary documents, which is often not an easy task with an author working in Maine. Bob Biersack of the Federal Election Commission's Data Systems Division answered numerous questions about the information available on public financing and generously shared his expertise on the income tax checkoff data. As always, Chuck Lakin and Sunny Pomerleau of the Colby College library enthusiastically helped me to locate sources and materials.

My research assistant, Beth Hermanson, compiled some of the statistics for the tables and appendixes. Erik Belenky and William Charron read earlier versions of the first three chapters and offered a number of thoughtful suggestions. I am especially indebted to Patricia Kick, who helped complete the manuscript under tight deadlines. Greg Anrig of the Twentieth Century Fund also deserves special thanks for his editorial assistance and efforts in preparing the manuscript for final publication.

INTRODUCTION

In the early 1970s, Congress responded to the political pressures generated by spiraling campaign costs and the financial abuses associated with the 1972 election by adopting a series of sweeping campaign finance reforms. These reforms were designed to resolve, once and for all, the problems inherent in a private system of financing elections. The hallmark of this ambitious effort was the Federal Election Campaign Act of 1974, a revised version of a 1971 statute that completely restructured the campaign finance system. This legislation required full public disclosure of the financial activities of federal candidates, set strict limits on political contributions, and established spending ceilings for presidential primary and general election campaigns. It also created a bipartisan agency, the Federal Election Commission, to enforce and administer the law.

The most innovative aspect of the Federal Election Campaign Act (FECA) was the creation of a public financing program for presidential primary and general election campaigns. At the time of its passage, public financing was heralded as the most significant reform of the campaign finance system in American history. Public funding, advocates claimed, would eliminate the undue influence of large contributions in presidential elections, enhance the role of small donors, reduce the emphasis placed on fundraising by candidates, limit campaign spending, and provide presidential aspirants with the funds needed to communicate their views to the electorate. Public financing would thus produce a more representative selection process, more substantive political campaigns, and more competitive presidential contests.

The FECA provided public money at every stage of the presidential selection process. For primary elections, the act established a voluntary program of partial public subsidies. Candidates who fulfilled certain eligibility requirements and agreed to abide by legally mandated spending limits would receive public funds on a dollar-for-dollar basis on the first $250 contributed by an individual, up to a maximum of half of the set spending limit. For general elections, the act set forth a voluntary program of full public funding for nominees of the major parties and a scheme of proportionate financing for minor party or new party candidates. The legislation also established public subsidies for national party nominating conventions. The revenues for the program were to come from the Presidential Election Campaign Fund, a separate federal account administered by the Department of the Treasury, which is funded through a tax checkoff option on federal income tax forms.

As the reformers anticipated, public subsidies have become a major source of revenue in presidential campaigns. Since 1976, the first election conducted under the act, the Presidential Election Campaign Fund has provided more than $660 million to eighty-three candidates and party nominating conventions.[1] Only one major party candidate, Republican John Connally in 1980, has refused to accept public money, while every major party presidential nominee has accepted such funding. Minor parties have also benefited from the program, including one independent presidential candidate, John Anderson, who qualified for a proportionate share of the general election subsidy in 1980.

After only five elections, the public financing system appeared to be on the verge of collapse. Rising costs and declining revenues had left the Presidential Election Campaign Fund on the brink of insolvency after the 1992 election. To avoid the financial collapse of the program, Congress adjusted the amount an individual may contribute to the Fund from one dollar to three dollars as part of the 1993 budget package. While this reform will provide a temporary solution to the program's financial difficulties, it will not resolve the major problems that confront the public financing system. Public enthusiasm, as well as congressional support for the program, has ebbed, and participation in the income tax checkoff, which is the program's sole source of revenue, has dropped sharply. Campaign staffs have developed creative accounting schemes that have minimized the law's ability to restrict spending, since they allow candidates to circumvent the law's contribution and expenditure limits. Public funding has also been undermined by the rise of "soft money," which is the popular term for donations raised outside of the contribution limits imposed on candidates. This source of funding has been especially detrimental since it has allowed the influence of wealthy interests to creep back into the contests for our nation's highest office.

The most acute problem facing the system in recent years has been a projected lack of adequate funding. In 1992, the program barely avoided a relatively minor shortfall that would have affected the revenues available to primary candidates. Following the election, the Federal

Election Commission estimated that the Fund would be $75 million to $100 million short of the amount needed to finance the 1996 presidential election. Such a shortfall would mean that only the grants for the national party conventions would be fully funded in 1996. General election candidates would receive only partial funding and no public subsidies would be available for primary campaigns.[2]

In an effort to avoid this possibility, Congress included a provision in the Fiscal Year 1994 budget resolution to increase the amount of the income tax checkoff from one dollar to three dollars for single filers and from a maximum of two dollars to six dollars for joint filers. This change, which was originally adopted in June 1993 as 'part of the Senate's version of the budget plan on a 55-43 vote and incorporated into the president's budget plan that was passed in August, should provide ample revenues to meet the costs of the public funding program for the next few elections.[3] It does not, however, guarantee the long-term financial health of the program. Nor does it resolve the many other problems that currently plague the system. These objectives can only be achieved through broader campaign finance reform legislation.

Congress has held a number of hearings and considered a variety of bills in recent years to address the problems that have arisen under the public financing scheme. No action has been taken, however, largely because of the controversial nature of the experience with public funding.

The salutary effects of public financing, which were once widely assumed, are now the subject of intense debate. Critics contend that the reforms have failed to fulfill their objectives and argue that the system of financing presidential elections is increasingly characterized by the kinds of abuses that were emblematic of the pre-Watergate period. Supporters, on the other hand, while admitting that further changes are needed to correct some of the unintended consequences of the reforms, claim that the law has achieved its most important objectives and demonstrated the value of substituting public resources for private sources of funding.

Sifting through the arguments on both sides of this debate is a complicated task. Some claims are predicated on widely held assumptions that have not been subjected to detailed analyses; others are based on detailed analyses that are subject to widely varying interpretations. The terms of the debate are complex because the regulations governing presidential campaign financing are complex: the present system is a patchwork of guidelines established by different statutes, court rulings, and administrative decisions. These provisions seek to achieve diverse objectives, which at times tend to conflict or compete with one another. The effects of the regulations are also complex. Some of the problems that plague the system are the result of structural flaws in the law. Others are consequences that were wholly unintended. Some are the result of efforts to accommodate valid, yet conflicting, regulatory goals, while others are the manifestations of the ever-changing dynamics of political finance and the inventiveness of political practitioners.

Given the complexity of the issues involved, it is not surprising that there is no consensus regarding the merits of public funding. This method of financing thus continues to demand the attention of scholars, legislators, and political observers alike, especially since it stands at the center of current legislative discussions on the regulation of political finance.

President Clinton and many congressional leaders support public funding. The merits of this approach have been debated in a number of recent congresses and the 103rd Congress is considering yet another proposal to reform the presidential system and extend public subsidies to House and Senate campaigns. With campaign finance reform once again high on the congressional agenda, it is an appropriate time to review the experience with public funding at the national level. Although this study is not intended to be a comprehensive review of the present system, it explores some of the major developments in the public financing program in an effort to improve our understanding of the effects of the law and highlight some of the major issues in the debate. It also seeks to provide a foundation for assessing alternatives for further reform and the future direction of campaign finance regulation.

BACKGROUND

Since the 1976 election, the financing of presidential campaigns has been governed by the provisions of the Federal Election Campaign Act of 1971 and the amendments to it adopted in 1974, 1976, and 1979.[4] These statutes were the result of a reform impulse that swept through the Congress in the early 1970s, an attitude spurred by growing concern over the role of money in federal elections. Rapidly rising campaign costs, an alarming increase in the role of wealthy contributors, and the financial abuses revealed by the investigations of the 1972 election combined to generate a popular outcry for reform. Congress responded to this demand for change by adopting a comprehensive scheme for the regulation of campaign finance.

From the mid-1950s to the early 1970s, campaign costs had skyrocketed, largely as a result of the increased role of media advertising in political campaigns. In the 1956 elections, the amount spent on political campaigns at all levels was estimated at $155 million. By 1968, total spending had grown to $300 million and then rose sharply to $425 million in 1972, or almost three times the amount spent sixteen years earlier.[5] The costs of presidential contests rose at an even more rapid rate.

Dwight Eisenhower and Adlai Stevenson spent a total of $11.6 million in the 1956 election. In 1972, Richard Nixon spent a staggering $61.4 million, more than twice the amount he spent in 1968, and George McGovern spent approximately $30 million, or almost three times the amount spent by Hubert Humphrey four years earlier.[6] The 1972 election thus cost more than eight times the 1956 contest, and spending seemed likely to continue to increase dramatically in the future.

Higher spending, in turn, led to a greater emphasis on fundraising since it forced candidates to devote extensive time to soliciting the funds needed to fuel their campaigns. In an effort to ease this burden, yet continue to generate the enormous sums needed to finance their campaigns, candidates increasingly relied on wealthy donors, or "fat cats," as their primary source of campaign gifts. In 1952, 110 individuals contributed $10,000 or more to a political candidate for a total of $1.9 million. In 1972, 1,254 individuals contributed $10,000 or more, including a number of individuals who each gave more than a million dollars to the candidate of their choice, for a total of more than $51.3 million. In addition, the number of individuals giving $500 or more rose from 9,500 in 1952 to 51,230 in 1972.[7]

This growing dependence on large contributions raised fundamental concerns about the health of the campaign finance system. Critics claimed that a system permitting such large gifts undermined the integrity of the political process by encouraging the widespread appearance of corruption, promoted intolerable inequities in the relative influence of individual citizens on electoral outcomes, exacerbated the role of special interests in politics, and led to enormous disparities in the resources available to candidates. These issues became a focal point of congressional and public attention after the 1972 election as the Watergate investigations revealed that the Nixon campaign had accepted a number of extraordinarily large gifts, solicited illegal donations from corporations and foreign interests, and promised ambassadorial appointments and legislative favors in exchange for campaign contributions.[8]

The FECA contained a number of provisions designed to ensure the integrity of the presidential campaign finance system and prevent the abuses exposed in the aftermath of the 1972 election. It addressed the problems associated with large gifts by placing a limit on campaign contributions. The law set a ceiling of $1,000 per election on the amount an individual can contribute to a presidential candidate and limited an individual's total annual contributions to all federal elections to $25,000. Political action committees (PACs) were allowed to give no more than $5,000 per election with no annual aggregate limit. The act also stipulated that a candidate may personally contribute no more than $50,000 to his or her own campaign.

To restrain the growth in expenditures and equalize the potential resources available to candidates, the law imposed a set of stringent spending ceilings on presidential campaigns. Different ceilings were applied to each stage of the selection process. All of the limits, which were established by the 1974 legislation with 1974 as their base year, were indexed to account for increases in the Consumer Price Index. (For a list of the specific limits applied in each election, see Appendix 1.)

An aggregate limit of $10 million per candidate was established for the primary campaign; with the adjustments for inflation, this amount had risen to $27.6 million in 1992. Each candidate was also allowed to spend an amount equal to 20 percent of this overall ceiling for fundraising, since it was assumed that the new regulations would force candidates to incur higher fundraising costs due to the need to finance their campaigns through smaller donations. In addition, the act established state-by-state expenditure ceilings so that relatively unknown candidates would have an opportunity to compete effectively against better-known or better-financed candidates in individual states.[9] These limits were set at the higher amount of either sixteen cents times the voting age population of the state or $200,000.

For convention and general election expenditures, the act established aggregate limits. The ceiling for convention spending was originally set at $2 million. This base amount was raised under the 1979 FECA Amendments to $3 million, and again to $4 million under a bill adopted in 1984.[10] In the general election, each candidate is allowed to spend $20 million; with adjustments for inflation, this amount had increased to $55.2 million by 1992. In addition, the national party committee of each of the presidential nominees is allowed to spend an amount equal to two cents times the voting age population in "coordinated spending" to help elect its candidate.

While limiting contributions and expenditures, the FECA also recognized the necessity of guaranteeing that adequate resources were available to presidential candidates. The act thus created a program of voluntary public financing for each stage of the presidential selection process. Funds were made available to all candidates, including minor party challengers, so long as they fulfilled certain eligibility and regulatory requirements.

For the primary election, the act established public matching funds for candidates who fulfill certain eligibility requirements and agree to adhere to the spending limits. In order to qualify, a candidate has to raise at least $5,000 in contributions of $250 or less in at least twenty states. Qualified candidates are then eligible to receive public monies on a dollar-for-dollar basis on the first $250 received from an individual, provided that the contribution was received after January 1 of the year before the election year. The maximum amount a candidate may receive in such payments is half of the overall spending limit, or $5 million under the original provisions of the act.

Although the 1974 law contained clear guidelines concerning the requirements to qualify for matching funds, it was less forthcoming as to when a qualified candidate's eligibility ended. This raised the concern that the availability of public funds may serve to encourage a losing candidate to remain in a race. Accordingly, the 1976 FECA Amendments modified the regulations and established the "ten percent rule." This rule stipulated that a presidential candidate who receives less than 10 percent of the vote in two consecutive primaries in which he or she is qualified for the ballot is ineligible for additional payments. The subsidies are restored if that candidate receives 20 percent of the vote in a later primary. The law also required that candidates who withdraw from the nomination race after receiving matching funds must return any remaining monies to the Treasury.[11]

In the general election, major party candidates are eligible for a flat grant equal to the full amount authorized by the spending limit. A "major party candidate" is legally defined as a candidate whose party received at least 25 percent of the vote in the previous election. A candidate qualifies for this grant upon receiving the party's nomination and consenting to certain legal and procedural requirements, which include accepting the spending limit and refusing to accept private contributions. Minor party candidates, which include candidates whose parties received at least 5 percent of the vote in the previous election, are eligible for a pro-rated subsidy under the law. The size of the subsidy is determined on the basis of the proportion of the vote the party received in the prior election calculated in comparison to the average vote of the major parties.[12] New parties, including independent candidates, and minor parties may also qualify for post-election subsidies on the same proportional basis if their percentage of the vote entitles them to public money for the first time or to a larger subsidy than the amount resulting from their vote in the previous election.

The major parties are also eligible for a flat grant equal to the full amount of the spending limit for their respective national nominating conventions, provided that they refuse to raise private contributions and adhere to the spending limit. These funds are usually issued by the Treasury in the summer of the year before the election year so that the parties can begin to make necessary arrangements. Since these amounts are needed prior to the election year, the law gives top funding priority to these payments.[13] A minor party may also qualify for convention funding, based on the same pro-rated distribution established for general election funds.

Revenues for the public financing program come from the voluntary checkoff provision on individual federal income tax returns that was established by the Revenue Act of 1971.[14] Individuals with federal tax liability were given the opportunity to designate one dollar (or two dollars on a joint return) to the Presidential Election Campaign Fund, a separate account in the U.S. Treasury, without increasing their tax obligation or reducing the amount of any refund. Monies from this account are then used to pay for the subsidies given to candidates and party organizations.

The public financing program is therefore "the lone historical example of Congress determining the size of an appropriation not by the needs of a program, but by what in essence is a yearly public referendum."[15] This unique form of funding originated from a proposal made by former Senator Russell Long (D-LA), who drafted a plan of public financing in 1966 designed to reduce the influence of wealthy donors and base the financing of presidential campaigns on the principle of "one person, one vote." Long's idea was to give each party one dollar in government funds for each vote received by the party's presidential candidate. The amounts received by the parties were to be used to pay the expenses associated with the presidential general election campaign.[16] This plan, according to Long, would "act as an inducement to the voter since his vote would not only select his candidate, but would help his candidate to pay for the expense of running for office."[17]

One of the drawbacks to Long's proposal was that it would have provided a larger subsidy to the Democrats, since the party had received more votes than the Republicans in the 1964 Johnson-Goldwater contest and was expected to outpoll the Republicans again in 1968. The Senate Finance Committee thus amended the bill to provide for a more equitable distribution of funds yet fulfill the basic objectives Long had outlined. The committee passed a plan that would allow taxpayers to designate one dollar of their tax liability to a Presidential Election Campaign Fund, which would provide a subsidy to each of the major parties at the rate of one dollar per vote based on an equal division of the total number of votes received by parties polling more than 10 million votes each.[18] At the time, Long noted that the proposal did not strictly fulfill the "one person, one vote" principle since it would exclude those voters who had no tax liability.[19] He acknowledged, however, that the bill was "the best we can do for the moment" and further stated that "if we pass this provision, and begin moving in that direction . . . with time we can improve on it and make it a better measure."[20]

The Senate Finance Committee's tax checkoff plan was initially adopted as an amendment to the Foreign Investors Tax Act of 1966, but it was effectively terminated before becoming operative in 1967. Four years later, when Congress again considered campaign finance reform legislation, the proposal was resurrected and adopted as part of the Revenue Act of 1971, following a bitter partisan debate dominated by the approaching presidential election. As enacted, the law slightly modified the 1966 law by allowing a taxpayer to earmark a checkoff contribution to the candidate of a specified party or direct that it be placed in a nonpartisan general account. Implementation of this provision was delayed until 1973, however, in order to avoid a threatened veto by President Nixon.

Before establishing the program in 1973, Congress made two changes to simplify its administration and promote public participation. Through an amendment to legislation continuing a temporary debt ceiling, the option of earmarking a contribution to a specific party was repealed and the Internal Revenue Service was directed to place the checkoff in a visible location on federal tax forms. The party provision was no longer considered necessary since subsidies were to be awarded equally to the parties based on the provisions of the FECA, which provided full grants to the major parties equal to the specified spending ceiling. The role of parties as prospective recipients of government subsidies was then diminished with the passage of the 1974 FECA amendments, which awarded subsidies directly to candidates and extended coverage to primary elections with the matching funds program. No additional major changes were made in the checkoff program until 1993, when Congress increased the amount of the voluntary designation as part of the President's budget package.

CURRENT ISSUES

In many ways, public funding was established as the linchpin of the political finance system created by the reforms of the 1970s. The program was designed to promote most of the objectives sought by the advocates of reform. In theory, public financing reduces the emphasis on fundraising and allows candidates to devote more time to the substantive aspects of a campaign by replacing private monies with public resources. The law seeks to diminish or eliminate the need to rely on wealthy donors and interest groups, thus minimizing the opportunities available to donors to influence candidates. This, in turn, helps guard against public perceptions of favoritism and the appearance of corruption in the political system, which can lead to public cynicism and alienation.

Public financing also helps to equalize the potential resources available to candidates so that serious challengers will have the funds needed to present themselves and their ideas to the electorate. The program is designed to broaden political participation by opening the process to candidates without ready access to personal resources and wealthy donors, and by encouraging candidates to solicit small contributions and expand their base of donors. Further, it provides an inducement to help control campaign spending by tying eligibility for subsidies to the acceptance of spending limits, a link that was reaffirmed by the Supreme Court's 1976 decision in *Buckley v. Valeo*, which declared that spending limits were constitutional when imposed on candidates receiving public subsidies.[21]

Proponents of public financing argue that the system has achieved most of these objectives. Since 1976, the program has encountered few administrative problems and has provided more than enough money to cover the subsidies granted to primary and general election candidates, and to the major parties for their national nominating conventions. It has gained widespread acceptance among presidential candidates and, according to these advocates, it has fulfilled much of its promise. Representative Al Swift (D-WA), chair of the House Subcommittee on Elections and a supporter of the reforms, summarized this position in a recent legislative hearing on the program:

> The [public financing] system has worked extremely well since its inception 15 years ago, and the goals for which it was designed have largely been achieved. Presidential candidates have been freed from the rigors of fund-raising. Campaign spending has been capped. Disclosure has been much improved. Incumbents and challengers have been placed on an even financial footing. Million dollar corporate donations in brown paper bags are a thing of the past [and] . . . . citizen participation in our election process has been dramatically increased.[22]

Similarly, Susan Lederman, President of the League of Woman Voters, has observed that public funding "is the cleanest money in American politics today." "This is financing," she says, "with 'no strings attached.' This is financing without the inappropriate association of special interest influence. This is financing that serves only the broad interests of *all* the voters."[23]

Critics present a radically different view of the program. Senator Mitch McConnell (R-KY), perhaps the leading congressional opponent of public funding, contends that "the expenditure limits and public financing imposed by the Federal Election Campaign Act of 1974 have created a regulatory disaster, where grassroots volunteers have been replaced by lawyers and accountants, candidates break the law with impunity, and wealthy contributors feed millions of dollars through innumerable backdoor accounts." [24] In defending their position that the program has failed, opponents cite a litany of problems. Among the most important are:

THE TAX CHECKOFF: Since 1981, public participation in the tax checkoff has steadily declined to a point where, in 1992, less than one out of five taxpayers agreed to designate a dollar of their tax payment to the Presidential Election Campaign Fund. Conversely, more than 60 percent of taxpayers expressly noted that they did not want a dollar of their payment to be given to this program. As a result, the monies deposited in the Fund have steadily declined, raising questions as to whether the program will be able to meet the costs of presidential campaigns in the future. Critics contend that the checkoff represents a national referendum on the issue of public funding and that the decline in participation demonstrates that the public has overwhelmingly rejected this notion of "welfare for politicians."[25]

CANDIDATE ELIGIBILITY: Under the provisions of the FECA, public subsidies are granted to any candidate who meets the eligibility requirements. Critics charge that the effect of the law has been to spur "fringe" candidates, such as convicted felon Lyndon LaRouche, and will continue to fund such candidates in the future. Taxpayers are thus forced to give their tax dollars to qualifying candidates who they may adamantly oppose or who represent the views of only a minor faction in the electorate.

SPENDING LIMITS: The ceilings on expenditures have failed to stop the increase in campaign spending. Instead of restraining candidates, the limits have proven to be little more than parchment barriers that are easily circumvented. In each election since the act was established, enterprising candidates have discovered ways to spend millions of dollars outside the law's parameters. The primary effect of these regulations has thus been to encourage presidential aspirants to pursue strategies designed to undermine the system. Such practices serve to enhance public cynicism and a loss of faith in the electoral process.

CONTRIBUTION LIMITS: The law has also failed to stem the flow of large contributions and special interest money into presidential campaigns. In particular, the rise of "soft money" has facilitated a return of "fat cat" contributions, as well as donations from corporations and labor union treasuries, two sources that had long been prohibited from giving money to federal candidates. In the 1988 election alone, hundreds of donations of $100,000 or more were received by the major parties to supplement the monies given to candidates through the public financing program. The growth of soft money has thus made a farce of the FECA's limits and fostered a resurrection of the sorts of financial abuses that characterized elections in the pre-reform era.

Have the reforms failed? Are the problems that have emerged so intractable or fundamental that the current system should be scrapped? Or are advocates correct in claiming that public financing has proven its value and that what is needed is further reform to build on the foundation established by the FECA? Should reform follow the current regulatory scheme or are new approaches needed? To answer these questions, each of the major problems identified by critics, as well as the benefits cited by supporters, needs to be explored.

These issues are interwoven throughout the analysis that follows in an effort to highlight the major issues in the public funding debate. Each aspect of the public financing program will be examined to identify what has worked and what has not worked in our nation's initial attempt to implement this innovative approach to electoral finance. This analysis begins by exploring the experience with the tax checkoff as a source of funding. Chapter Two looks at the role of public subsidies in the pre-nomination campaign and documents how these subsidies have influenced candidate fundraising strategies and the ways candidates have adapted their approaches to accommodate the FECA's restrictions on contributions and spending. Chapter Three reviews the financing of general election campaigns and focuses on the issues raised by the advent of soft money as a source of funding in presidential campaigns. The final chapter assesses various proposals for reform and offers legislative recommendations for improving the campaign finance system in the years to come.

CHAPTER ONE

FINANCING PUBLIC FINANCING

I n February 1991, a year before the citizens of New Hampshire cast their
ballots in the nation's first presidential primary, FEC Chairman John
Warren McGarry predicted that the public financing program would
face a severe shortfall of funds in the upcoming election. This deficit,
he warned, could "affect campaign strategies, create unnecessary hard-
ships and inequities, and . . . induce some candidates to reject public funding altogether."[1] The possibility of inadequate funding was considered
so likely that the Department of the Treasury and the Federal Election
Commission adopted new regulations to cover this eventuality. The rules
required, in part, that the amounts due candidates in matching fund payments be reduced proportionally if the funds were not available for the
full subsidy, or not be paid at all if there was not enough money available to provide full payments for the conventions and general election.[2]

Although initially projected at $15 million,[3] the anticipated 1992
deficit was narrowly avoided due to a number of unexpected circumstances.
The contest for the Democratic nomination got off to a relatively late
start since many of the party's most prominent potential candidates were
hesitant to enter the race given President Bush's popularity in the aftermath of the Gulf War. Most of those who did enter declared their candidacies less than seven months before the New Hampshire primary and
raised significantly less money than their counterparts in previous elections. While President Bush was widely perceived as the probable winner of the 1992 election throughout 1991, he also raised less than
expected prior to the New Hampshire primary since he did not begin
aggressively raising funds early. In addition, the rate of inflation fell below

initial estimates, which reduced the amount needed for the conventions and general election. Finally, the program received more money than expected because checkoff receipts did not decline as steeply as they had in previous election cycles.[4]

While the system dodged a bullet in 1992, it may not be so fortunate in the future. In December 1992, the FEC estimated that in 1996 the program would need about $24 million to pay for the national party conventions, about $120 million for the general election, and as much as $69 million for primary matching funds payments. The total amount needed, more than $200 million, was projected to be approximately $75 million more than the estimated sum that would be available from the Presidential Election Campaign Fund.[5]

The extent of the financial crisis was so severe that Congress was compelled to take action in 1993 by tripling the amount of the tax checkoff beginning in 1994. If this reform works as intended, the Fund should have adequate revenues to finance the 1996 election and perhaps a few subsequent campaigns. This change, however, is at best a short-term solution that will not necessarily guarantee the long-term financial security of the public funding program. To achieve this end, the causes of the Fund's financial instability must be identified and addressed.

Why did the financing of the public funding program break down? How effective will the checkoff be in the future? To answer these questions, a review of the experience with the checkoff is essential. This review must focus on the two major sources of the Fund's financial problems: the structural flaw in the law, which has led to a system characterized by rising costs but static contributions, and a decline in participation in the tax checkoff program. Ensuring the long-term health of the public funding program requires solving both of these problems.

THE FATAL FLAW

The level of taxpayer support is not the major source of the financial difficulties that have recently threatened the viability of the Presidential Election Campaign Fund. The primary reason why the Fund has not proven to be self-sustaining is what the FEC has described as "the fatal flaw" in the law: payments from the Fund are indexed for inflation, but the tax checkoff that finances the system is not.[6] As a result, the costs of the program increased significantly, while receipts from the tax checkoff did not.

The rising costs of the public financing program are noted in Table 1.1. As the figures indicate, the amount paid out of the Presidential Election Campaign Fund to cover the costs of the program grew from $72.3 million in the 1976 election to $174.4 million in 1992, an increase of

TABLE 1.1

PRESIDENTIAL ELECTION CAMPAIGN FUND PAYMENTS
($ MILLIONS)

	1976	1980	1984	1988	1992
Convention	4.4	8.8	16.2	18.4	22.1
General Election	43.6	58.9	80.8	92.2	110.5
Primary	24.3	31.5	36.5	67.5	41.8
TOTAL	$72.3	$99.2	$133.5	$178.1	$174.4

Source: Federal Election Commission.

more than 140 percent. The general election grants, which were set at
$40 million in 1974 ($20 million per candidate), grew from $43.6 million in 1976 to $110.5 million in 1992, or an increase of about 150 percent. The total for convention funding rose at an even greater rate, from
$4.4 million to $22.1 million. This 400 percent increase is larger than
the rise in general election costs because the original base amount, $2
million per party, has subsequently been altered twice to produce a new
base of $4 million per party beginning in 1984. Had these adjustments
not been made, $20 million less would have been paid out of the Fund
to finance conventions in recent elections.[7]

The rise in primary matching fund payments has been less predictable
because the costs of this part of the program are largely determined by the
number of candidates and the amount each raises in individual contributions
of $250 or less. The largest sum was paid out in the 1988 election, when
15 candidates received a total of $67.5 million. The maximum amount an
individual candidate may receive in matching funds, however, has steadily increased since this sum is equal to one-half of the primary spending limit,
which is also adjusted for inflation. Accordingly, the maximum payment
for which a candidate may qualify under the matching fund program has
risen from $5.4 million in 1976 to more than $13 million in 1992.[8]

In contrast, the amount an individual may contribute to the Presidential Election Campaign Fund was set at one dollar (or two dollars on
a joint return) when the program was established. John Surina, the
FEC's staff director, has noted that the dollar checked off in the 1976
election cycle was worth about 92 cents in 1974 dollars. By the 1992 cycle,
the purchasing power of this same dollar was worth about 36 cents. Consequently, the amount of the checkoff should have been increased to
about three dollars by 1992 in order to maintain its equivalent purchasing
power.[9] Even if the amount of the checkoff had been adjusted for inflation by being rounded *down* to the nearest whole dollar, and *even if these
adjustments were started as late as 1991*, the FEC estimates that the Presidential

Election Campaign Fund would have a surplus in the neighborhood of $140 million at the end of 1996, instead of facing a projected shortfall.[10]

Why the checkoff was not adjusted to keep pace with inflation is not clear from the legislative record. The outcome of this oversight, however, is a wholly unintended consequence of the law. When drafting the FECA, legislators could not have anticipated the high inflation of the late 1970s, which had a significant effect on program costs. For example, the general election payment rose by more than 80 percent between 1976 and 1984, as compared to an increase of less than 40 percent between 1984 and 1992. Some might argue that Congress could have avoided the current situation by correcting this problem when passing amendments to the FECA in 1976 and 1979. Yet, during this period, the program was still in its infancy, checkoff participation was rising, and the potential long-term consequences of the law had not become evident.

What is clear is that this imbalance between payments and contributions is the primary source of the recent financial concerns associated with the Presidential Election Campaign Fund. This is demonstrated by the estimates provided in Table 1.2, which presents the status of the Fund (that is, the amount received annually from the checkoff, the sums spent annually, and the yearly balance) if taxpayer participation had remained at its highest level—the 1981 rate of 28.7 percent. The estimates also assume a continued low inflation rate of 4.0 percent per annum for the years after 1992. Even under these best-case conditions, the figures show that the Fund would not have had the revenues to finance the projected costs of the election in 2004. In that year, the Fund would have faced an estimated shortfall of $48.2 million. So, even if participation had not fallen, the Fund would have made it through only two more elections before running out of money.

Now that Congress has raised the amount of the checkoff, financial insolvency will be avoided in 1996. But the structural flaw in the legislation has not been corrected. Congress simply increased the amount of the checkoff; it did not index it to account for the effects of inflation. Consequently, the public funding program will once again face a financial imbalance in future elections. For example, if inflation continues at its current low rate, an upward adjustment in the dollar amount of the checkoff would probably be necessary prior to the election in 2000 if the checkoff contribution is to maintain its purchasing power. Without such adjustments, the long-term viability of the Fund can not be assured.

THE DECLINE IN PARTICIPATION

The inevitable deficit in the public financing program was due to arrive in 1996, not 2004, because the financial problems of the Fund have been

Table 1.2

PRESIDENTIAL ELECTION CAMPAIGN FUND
ESTIMATED ACTIVITY WITH HIGH PARTICIPATION, 1980–2000

Calendar Year	Checkoff Receipts[a] ($)	COLA Adjustment[b] (%)	Disbursements ($)	Year End Balance[c] ($)
1980	38,838,417		101,427,115	73,752,205
1981	41,049,052		630,255	114,373,289
1982	41,480,941		1,070	155,911,559
1983	42,256,679		11,796,485	186,393,652
1984	42,428,482		120,149,768	109,178,173
1985	43,315,488		1,617,841	150,937,659
1986	44,614,570		5,596	195,608,273
1987	44,507,413		17,784,000	222,688,993
1988	45,119,115		158,560,804	109,350,803
1989	46,099,404	2.51	1,843,017	153,629,215
1990	47,054,924	2.65	0	200,761,503
1991	47,571,848	2.76	21,200,000	227,728,770
1992	47,995,010	2.85	153,191,151	123,096,707
1993	48,795,010	2.96	2,212,118	170,181,599
1994	49,595,010	3.10	55,000	219,721,609
1995	50,395,010	3.24	24,779,040	245,337,579
1996	51,195,010	3.38	188,506,547	108,026,042
1997	51,995,010	3.53	2,568,029	157,933,023
1998	52,795,010	3.69	55,000	210,673,033
1999	53,595,010	3.86	29,549,466	234,718,577
2000	54,395,010	4.03	239,454,515	49,659,072
2001	55,195,010	4.22	3,086,273	102,267,809
2002	55,995,010	4.40	55,000	158,207,819
2003	56,795,010	4.60	35,238,288	179,764,541
2004	57,595,010	4.81	285,553,963	(48,194,412)

[a] The figures for 1980 and 1981 represent the actual activity in the Fund. The estimates for 1982 through 1992 are derived from actual proceeds with adjustments estimating deposits if participation remained at the 1981 high of 28.7 percent. The estimates for 1993 through 2004 assume 28.7 percent participation and an average growth in the number of taxpayers based on previous patterns.

[b] The actual CPI is used for 1980 to 1989, with an annual increase of 4.0 percent assumed for the years after 1992.

[c] The year-end balance includes repayments as well as checkoff receipts. Actual repayments through 1992 are figured into this amount and estimates are included for the years 1992 through 2004.

Source: Federal Election Commission.

exacerbated by a decline in the level of checkoff participation. This decline is one of the most hotly debated aspects of the presidential campaign finance system. Critics claim that the experience with the checkoff provides the best evidence to date of the public's attitude toward public financing. Rather than embracing this concept, taxpayers have taken advantage of the opportunity to express their views and conclusively voted against the program. Representative Bob Livingston, a Republican from Louisiana, for example, argues that "the American people have rejected the system; fewer than 20 percent of them support it. That means that 80 percent do not support it."[11]

Supporters, such as Fred Wertheimer of Common Cause and Susan Lederman of the League of Women Voters, contend that the checkoff has significantly broadened the base of participation in the financing of presidential campaigns.[12] They note that the number of people who contribute through the checkoff, even if only one out of five taxpayers, is notably higher than the number of individuals who usually give money to campaigns and is evidence of a strong public commitment. They further contend that the problem with the checkoff is that most taxpayers lack an understanding of the program, and argue that if the public was given more information, participation would increase. Critics challenge this assumption, noting instead that additional information will only increase the number of non-participants. Indeed, Thomas Schatz, a leader of the nonprofit group, Citizens Against Government Waste, has concluded: "The more taxpayers find out about the Presidential Election Campaign Fund, the less interested they are in checking the box on their tax return."[13]

These arguments and the viability of the tax checkoff as a form of financing have been difficult to assess due to the lack of detailed information concerning the experience with the checkoff. On both sides of the debate, the most commonly cited statistic is the percentage of taxpayers who participate in the checkoff. This percentage, which is determined by the Internal Revenue Service (IRS), is based on the ratio of all returns that have marked the "yes" box on the checkoff to all individual returns filed that year. Yet these figures, which represent the government's official tabulation on checkoff participation and are reported by the FEC, offer little insight into the operation of the program.[14]

First, the FEC reports on checkoff participation do not include the number of individual tax returns processed each year or the number of actual participants. Without this information, it is hard to determine the extent to which participation has actually declined. It may be the case that the number of returns has increased, but the number of participants has remained static or increased at a lower rate, thus producing a drop in the rate of participation but no actual decline in the number of participants. Second, the usual figures do not distinguish between taxpayers with a tax liability and those without a liability. This is a crucial consideration. Under the laws governing the checkoff, a dollar is designated to the Presidential Election Campaign Fund only from those taxpayers who check "yes" on the tax form and have a tax liability.[15] No revenue is produced by those taxpayers who check "yes" but have no tax liability. Accordingly, the decline in the Fund's annual revenues may be influenced by changes in tax liability or by the participation of taxpayers without a liability, rather than by a simple decline in participation. Third, these figures provide no information on non-participants. Are these taxpayers active non-participants, that is, individuals who check the "no" box on their tax forms? Or are they passive, simply leaving the boxes blank? Finally, they provide no insight at all into who participates and who does not.[16] As these criticisms indicate, a more detailed understanding of the experience with the tax checkoff is needed if some of the major issues in the campaign finance debate are to be unraveled.

The most notable development in the tax checkoff program since its adoption is the steady decline in participation that began in the early 1980s. The early years of the program were characterized by rising participation and substantial growth in the annual revenues deposited into the Presidential Election Campaign Fund (see Table 1.3). These trends peaked in 1981, when the FEC reported that a high of 28.7 percent of all returns included a contribution to the Fund. Since then, participation has steadily fallen to a low of 17.7 percent in 1992. The number of returns designating monies to the Fund, according to IRS estimates, has dropped from 27 million to approximately 20.5 million. Annual receipts have declined from a high of roughly $41 million in 1981 to less than $30 million in 1992.

The decline in participation has not been as drastic as is often assumed. While the rate of participation has steadily declined since 1981, the actual number of participants has not. Between 1983 and 1991, a period when the rate of participation fell from 24.2 percent to 19.5 percent, the actual number of returns that included a contribution remained relatively stable, ranging from 23.2 million to 22.3 million. Nor has the decline been consistent. In three of the past seven years (1986, 1988, and 1990), the number of participants was actually higher than in the previous year. This suggests that the sharpness of the decline that is often reported is not simply due to the number of participants; it is also a function of the increase that has occurred in the number of tax returns filed each year. For example, in 1985, 22.8 million taxpayers supported the program, yielding a participation rate of 23.0 percent. In 1988, the same number of taxpayers checked "yes" but the percentage rate fell to 21.0 percent. The combination of lower participation and a growth in the number of taxpayers has thus produced the appearance of a steeper drop in participation than has actually taken place.

TABLE 1.3

THE FEDERAL INCOME TAX CHECKOFF, 1972–1992[a]

Calendar Year	Total Number of Returns (Millions)	Total Number with Checkoff (Millions)	Percent of Returns with Checkoff	Dollar Amount Designated
1992	N/A	20.5	17.7	29,592,735
1991	114.1	22.3	19.5	32,322,336
1990	112.5	22.4	19.8	32,462,979
1989	110.3	22.1	20.1	32,285,646
1988	107.0	22.8	21.0	33,013,987
1987	103.5	22.4	21.7	33,651,947
1986	102.4	23.9	23.0	35,753,837
1985	99.4	22.8	23.0	34,712,761
1984	96.3	22.9	23.7	35,036,761
1983	95.3	23.2	24.2	35,631,068
1982	95.5	25.7	27.0	39,023,882
1981	94.0	27.0	28.7	41,049,052
1980	93.1	25.3	27.4	38,838,417
1979	90.8	23.2	25.4	35,941,347
1978	87.4	24.9	28.6	39,246,689
1977	85.6	23.2	27.5	36,606,008
1976	82.5	21.2	25.5	33,731,945
1975	81.7	19.9	24.2	31,656,525
1974 [b]	78.9	—	—	27,591,546
1973 [c]	78.9	—	—	2,427,000

[a] The data on tax returns refer to the returns of the previous tax year, while the figures on the amount contributed to the Presidential Election Campaign Fund are based on the calendar year. For example, 20.5 million or 17.7 percent of the 1991 tax returns (which are filed in 1992) indicated a checkoff of one or two dollars to the Fund. These returns generated $29,592,735, which was deposited in the Fund during calendar year 1992.

[b] There may be slight variations between the participation rates listed and the rate determined by calculating the figures on the number of returns and number of returns with a checkoff. This variance is due to rounding and discrepancies that may occur in the figures reported to the FEC by the IRS, which usually only include the returns processed by June of the calendar year.

[c] The 1973 tax forms were the first to have the checkoff on the first page; in 1972, taxpayers had to file a separate form to exercise the checkoff option. To compensate for the presumed difficulty caused by the separate form in the previous year, taxpayers were allowed to designate one dollar for 1972 as well as for 1973 on the 1973 form. Given these circumstances, total and percentage figures for these returns would be misleading.

Source: Federal Election Commission, Annual Reports of the Commissioner of the Internal Revenue Service, and "Presidential Election Campaign Fund Checkoff," Memorandum from the Internal Revenue Service, Statistics of Income Division.

In addition to overstating the extent of the recent decline, the checkoff figures reported by the Internal Revenue Service (IRS) and FEC also underestimate the level of participation. The statistics commonly reported by the IRS are based on totals compiled on a fiscal year basis and usually include only returns processed by June of the report year.[17] These totals may significantly underestimate participation. Although only a few estimates based on broader time frames are available, these analyses indicate that participation is at least 12 to 15 percent higher than the common figures suggest.

For example, a few years ago, the IRS selectively sampled the 1985 tax returns to estimate state-by-state participation rates for the federal tax checkoff. This analysis determined that slightly more than 14 million returns nationwide checked one "yes" box and about 12.8 million returns checked two boxes, for a total of 26.8 million returns with at least one box checked or an estimated participation rate of about 26.2 percent.[18] In contrast, the reported figure for the 1985 tax year is 23.9 million returns and a participation rate of 23 percent.

In 1989, the IRS conducted a complete analysis of all returns filed in the 1988 tax year.[19] More than 25.7 million of the 109.7 million returns included in this analysis designated a contribution to the Presidential Election Campaign Fund. Of these, 14.5 million checked one box and about 11.2 million checked two boxes. The overall rate of participation was 23.5 percent. The usual figures cited for the 1988 returns are 22.1 million contributors and a participation rate of 20.1 percent.

Actual checkoff participation was therefore about 15 percent higher than the widely reported rate in 1985 and 1988. Whether this is true for all years can not be precisely determined due to the lack of comparable data. It would not be surprising, however, to find that participation is underreported in all years and that participation is higher than has been assumed. Certainly, this is the conclusion suggested by the information that is available.

These discrepancies between reported participation and actual participation raise another important issue: is the number of tax returns filed the best means of determining participation? A more accurate measure of public support may be to determine the number of *taxpayers represented* by the checkoff designations rather than the number of tax returns filed with a "yes" box marked. Most observers assume that the number of returns is synonymous with the number of taxpayers who support the program. This is not the case. Because of the role of joint returns, an emphasis on the number of returns always underrepresents the number of taxpayers that actually participate in the program. For example, the 25.7 million 1988 returns that included a checked "yes" box actually represented the preference of more than 37 million taxpayers, since those returns with two boxes checked represented the preference of at least two taxpayers.

The percentage of the taxpaying public that supports the program is there-fore significantly higher than the level implied by the percentage based on the number of returns.

Other studies of the tax checkoff have also noted that participation is higher than the level implied by the statistics related to tax returns. In a 1981 analysis of IRS data, Kim Quaile Hill estimated that 35 percent of *eligible* taxpayers (that is, those with a tax liability) contributed through the checkoff in 1977 and 38 percent did in 1978.[20] The figures distributed by the FEC for these years, which are based on tax returns, are 27.5 percent and 28.6 percent. Ruth Jones and Warren Miller, in a 1985 study of National Election Studies data, found that 31 percent of the *adult citizenry* reported contributing through the checkoff in 1979.[21] For the same year, Jack Noragon estimated that 39 percent of *eligible tax-payers* participated, as compared to the FEC's figure of 25.4 percent.[22] Jones later found that 30 percent of all adults said they gave through the check-off in 1982, 33 percent in 1984, and 30 percent in 1986.[23] Checkoff par-ticipation is therefore not nearly as low as critics have suggested. Indeed, at least through the mid-1980s, about one out of every three taxpayers was supporting the program.

Why comprehensive data on checkoff participation is not readily available is a subject of much speculation. One reason may be that Congress has not required the IRS to publish a detailed annual summary of checkoff activity and, without a mandate, the agency has not con-sidered such a report necessary. Another reason may be the fractured admin-istration of the program. No one agency has ultimate authority over the public financing program or access to all of the information relevant to its financing: the IRS is responsible for administering the checkoff, the Treasury Department supervises the Presidential Election Campaign Fund, and the FEC authorizes payments from the Fund and monitors the use of public money. In recent years the FEC has tried to acquire more information from the IRS and Treasury. While the Commission has had some success in gaining additional data, inter-agency divisions contin-ue to impede the achievement of a comprehensive understanding of check-off participation patterns.

THE DECLINE IN REVENUE

The tax checkoff has also experienced a decline in annual receipts. Most ob-servers have simply assumed that this outcome is a result of the drop in par-ticipation. The problem with this explanation is that the annual revenue loss does not correspond to the drop in participation. This suggests that there are other factors that have contributed to the Fund's financial problems.

Between 1983 and 1991, the number of returns designating a con-tribution to the Fund fell from 23.2 million to 22.3 million, and annual receipts fell from $35.6 million to $32.3 million. A decline of 900,000 returns is thus associated with an annual revenue loss of about $3.3 million. But under the terms of the program an individual may only contribute one dollar to the Fund and a joint filer may contribute up to two dollars. So even if every one of these 900,000 returns was a joint filing that checked off the legal maximum of two dollars, receipts should have declined by no more than $1.8 million, or $1.5 million less than the actual difference. Similarly, in 1986, the number of returns with a contribution rose by 1.1 million, but receipts increased by less than $1.1 million, or by less than the minimum of a dollar per participant.

The lack of detailed information about tax filings makes it impossible to determine the precise causes of the annual rise or decline in receipts. The IRS does not provide annual information on the number of participants who are single or joint filers or the number of joint filers who choose to contribute a dollar rather than two dollars. Some of the revenue discrepancies may therefore be due to annual changes in the composition of returns. For example, single filers may be replacing joint filers, or more joint filers may be checking one box instead of two. Such changes would produce less money, even if the actual number of returns designating a contribution was rising, since one dollar donors would be replacing two dollar donors.

Another likely explanation for the changing pattern of receipts is that some participants with tax liability, who are eligible to contribute to the Fund, are being replaced by participants with no tax liability, who may not contribute to the Fund. At the very least, it is possible that the proportion of participants with no tax liability may be on the rise. If this were the case, the overall number of participants could remain fairly stable, yet result in a significant loss of revenue, because the expressed preference of a growing percentage of taxpayers would not result in a tax dollar being deposited in the Fund. While it is not possible from the available data to determine whether such a pattern exists (the IRS does not release information annually on the number of returns without a tax liability or refund that exercise the checkoff), it can be shown that the tax status of participants has had a significant effect on the revenues of the public funding program. This is one of the conclusions to be drawn from Table 1.4.[24]

Although the IRS does not publish any sort of detailed analysis of the tax checkoff, the agency's Statistics of Income Division does have a slightly more refined breakdown of the final data from the 1988 tax returns than that provided in its published reports. These data, which are analyzed in Table 1.4, raise a number of important issues, while shedding light on some of the central controversies in the campaign finance debate.

The tax status of checkoff participants, at least in 1989, had a significant effect on the receipts deposited into the Presidential Election Campaign Fund. More than 25.7 million 1988 tax returns included a

TABLE 1.4

CHECKOFF PARTICIPATION, 1988 TAX YEAR

	All Returns	Returns with Tax Liability (Eligible)	Returns without Tax Liability (Not Eligible)
PARTICIPATION			
Total Number of Returns[a]	109,708,280	89,337,593	20,370,687
Total Number with Checkoff	25,759,758	21,434,266	4,325,492
One Box	14,510,942	11,483,790	3,027,152
Two Boxes	11,248,816	9,950,476	1,298,340
Percent of Total Returns with Checkoff	23.5	24.0	21.2
Percentage of Total Checkoff Returns	100.0	83.2	16.8
REVENUE			
Total Number of Boxes Checked[b]	37,008,574	31,384,742	5,623,832
Revenue to Fund ($)	31,384,742		
Potential Revenue ($) Lost via Ineligibility	5,623,832		

[a] Individual returns only.

[b] Calculated by adding the number of returns with one box checked and twice the number of returns with two boxes checked.

Source: Internal Revenue Service, Statistics of Income Division, Individual File, Unpublished Data, Tax Year 1988.

contribution to the Fund. Only 21.4 million of these returns, however, were filed by individuals with any tax liability. More than 4.3 million returns, or close to 17 percent of all the returns that designated a contribution to the Fund, were filed by individuals who had no tax liability. Of these, about 3 million were from single filers or from joint filers who checked only one box, and about 1.3 million were filed by joint filers who checked two boxes.[25]

To put it another way, more than 5.6 million taxpayers, represented by 4.3 million tax returns, expressed their desire to contribute to the Fund on their 1988 tax return but could not do so because they were technically not eligible to participate. These individuals were effectively disenfranchised from the system: their "vote" did not count and the government did not act on their request. As a result, the public financing program lost a significant amount of money. In 1989 alone, the Fund "lost" a potential $5.6 million in receipts due to the ineligibility of participants.

Changes in the tax laws and the tax status of individuals participating in the checkoff may therefore play a significant role in the financial decline of the Presidential Election Campaign Fund. For example, if the returns filed since 1988 were characterized by patterns similar to those of the 1988 tax year, an estimated $16 million to $20 million in potential receipts may have been lost over the past four years alone due to ineligible participants.[26] This is equivalent to about a quarter of the shortfall that was anticipated for 1996. When this estimate is combined with the additional $20 million in expenses that have been incurred by the Fund due to the statutory changes in the base amount provided for convention funding, almost half of the projected shortfall can be explained.

These projections may even underestimate the amount of money lost as a result of disenfranchised participants. One of the changes that has occurred since the adoption of the tax reforms of the mid-1980s is that the number of individuals without a tax liability has substantially increased. From 1980 to 1986, the estimated number of individual tax returns filed with the IRS rose from about 94 million to 103 million, an increase of slightly less than 10 percent. During this same period, the number of returns showing no tax liability declined from about 20 million to a low of 16.3 million, a drop of about 18 percent. Since then, the proportion of returns without a liability has steadily increased. Between 1986 and 1990 (the last year for which information is available), the estimated number of returns rose from 103 million to slightly more than 113 million, an increase of about 10 percent. Yet the number of returns without a liability grew at a much faster pace, from 16.3 million to about 24 million, a rise of almost 50 percent. Accordingly, by the 1990 tax year, more than one out of every five returns was filed by an individual or family who had no tax liability and thus was unable to designate a contribution to the Presidential Election Campaign Fund.[27]

Perhaps the meaning of these figures is best understood if placed in a different context. Congress recently adopted a "motor-voter" registration bill in an effort to improve participation in federal elections.

This law is designed to address what is widely considered to be one of the more serious problems in our democratic system, the problem of voter disenfranchisement as a result of an individual's failure or inability to register to vote. Numerous studies have shown that only about 70-80 percent of eligible voters are registered to vote and therefore eligible to participate. These studies also note that registration is the major barrier to voter participation.[28] The new legislation therefore seeks to improve participation by providing easier methods to register.

Similarly, only about 80 percent of all tax filers are eligible to participate in the tax checkoff because of their current tax status. The regulations governing contributions to the Presidential Election Campaign Fund have thus served to disenfranchise a significant portion of the American public from this component of our electoral system. Given the basic principle of "one person, one vote," which was the concept that gave rise to the notion of a checkoff, these individuals should be allowed to participate. At least, there is no theoretical reason to bar them from doing so. Their exclusion from the process is a result of the legal fiction upon which the checkoff is based: since these taxpayers have no tax liability in a given year, it is assumed that they "have" no dollar to give to the Fund. The public funding program, however, is a public good that is designed to benefit all taxpayers equally. As such, all those who file should be allowed to participate.

One reform of the system that should be considered, therefore, is to deposit a contribution into the Presidential Election Campaign Fund from any participant, regardless of their tax status. This would help to ensure that the basic principle of "one person, one vote" is more fully realized. It would also help to ease the financial pressures facing the Fund and improve participation since there are certainly individuals who are not participating in the checkoff due to their understanding of the law.

WHY HAS PARTICIPATION DECLINED?

While the decline in checkoff support is not as great as most have assumed, there has clearly been a drop-off in the number of participants. This is especially true for 1992. Only 20.5 million taxpayers designated a contribution to the Fund in that year, as compared to 22.3 million who did so in 1991. This represents the largest single-year drop in the number of participants in the checkoff's brief history. Whether this presages a period of substantial decline or another stage of leveling off remains to be seen.

Why participation has declined is a subject of great speculation and interest. There are almost as many theories advanced to explain this occurrence as there are observers of the process. Many attribute the drop-off to a collective decision made by millions of taxpayers who reject the notion of public funding either in principle or on the basis of more partisan or pragmatic concerns. Others claim that the ebb in participation does not represent an informed decision by non-participants at all. Instead, they claim just the opposite, and attribute the decrease to a lack of public awareness, inadequate understanding of the purposes of the program, and a rise in the number of taxpayers who do not remember the events and abuses that led to the adoption of the campaign finance reforms. Changing tax practices are also commonly cited as the culprit, especially the rise in the number of taxpayers who rely on paid preparers to complete their returns. Accountants are charged with failing to explain the checkoff option to their clients and using computer software packages that tend to reduce participation since they automatically default to "no" on the checkoff question. The decline may also bear little relation to attitudes toward public funding per se, but instead represent another manifestation of public cynicism toward the electoral process and popular dissatisfaction with the political system in general. All of these reasons contain some element of truth, yet none of them conclusively explains what has occurred.

The most common rationale advanced to explain decreasing participation is that taxpayers have rejected the system. The low level of participation is thus viewed as reflecting the attitudes of an increasingly large majority who have voted against public funding in what essentially constitutes a national referendum on the issue. These individuals have lost faith in the current system or oppose the idea of public financing because it subsidizes partisan activity they do not support, because they regard it to be an inappropriate limitation on political speech, or because they believe tax monies could be put to a better use than to provide subsidies to candidates. Senator McConnell of Kentucky has forcefully advanced this sort of argument, concluding that "the vast majority of Americans, who are fed up with taxes and irresponsible government spending, are in no mood to pay for anyone's political campaign and do not support the Presidential Election Campaign Fund."[29]

Does non-participation reflect opposition to public financing of campaigns? While critics of the program assume this to be true, other observers, especially supporters of the program, have argued that this is not the case. Supporters note that individuals who do not check "yes" on their tax forms may not be active opponents. That is, rather than checking "no," these individuals may simply leave the checkoff boxes blank. Non-participation may therefore reflect negligence, a lack of understanding of the law, or the lack of a clear opinion, rather than active opposition to the program.

Studies released by the IRS have demonstrated that a substantial portion of taxpayers are passive non-participants. These surveys, which are known as taxpayer utilization studies, provide estimates of the number of returns that make use of different features of the tax form based on statistical samples of about 10,000 returns. In recent years, the agency has shared the results of these surveys with the FEC so that the Commission can gain a better understanding of the experience with the checkoff program. The surveys show that the checkoff box is left blank on about 16 percent of all returns and that this percentage has increased slightly over the past two years (see Table 1.5). While these findings support the notion that all non-participants are not active opponents, they also indicate that the number of blank boxes is much lower than checkoff supporters have assumed, and that critics are correct in arguing that a majority of taxpayers actively refuse to participate in the program. But this does not confirm the further assumption that those who check "no" do so because they are opposed to public financing. While this is certainly a logical premise, supporters continue to argue that this opposition is at least in part an outcome of inadequate knowledge of the law.

Public opinion polls are usually a helpful resource for discerning public attitudes on policy issues. In the area of public financing, however, they offer few steadfast conclusions. Public responses to survey questions on public financing vary greatly, with results ranging from a majority in support of the notion to a majority firmly opposed to it, depending on the context and wording of the question asked.[30] Frank Sorauf, one of the leading experts on the campaign finance system, has reviewed the available public opinion data and concludes that the public attitude toward public funding is best described as "ambivalent." "All in all," he concludes,

TABLE 1.5

IRS SURVEYS OF TAXPAYER RESPONSE TO CHECKOFF QUESTION (%)

Response	1992 Returns	1991 Returns	1989 Returns
Left Box Blank	18.62	16.02	14.74
Checked "Yes"	21.00	20.99	24.67
Checked "No"	60.37	63.02	60.59

Note: These figures represent estimates based on selective samplings of returns. The 1989 results are based on samples of returns filed through September 1990. The 1991 and 1992 results are based on samples of returns filed through the beginning of May (N=9,723 and 8,987, respectively). Figures may not total 100 percent due to rounding.

Source: Federal Election Commission and Internal Revenue Service, "1992 Taxpayer Usage Study," Report No. 13, May 1993.

"there is probably a plurality, perhaps even a majority, for public financing combined with spending limits and/or the exclusion of private contributions—a majority, that is, for something like the public funding of presidential elections which less than 20 percent of the income tax filers support with a check mark. *Ambivalence* is perhaps too timid a word."[31]

General attitudes toward public financing, therefore, do not explain patterns of participation. While it is safe to assume that a significant percentage of those who check "no" oppose the program, opposition to the program is not the sole reason why people fail to contribute. Partisanship and ideological considerations may also influence participation. Since the Republicans as a party tend to oppose public financing and Republican leaders, especially in the Congress and state legislatures, have generally not given strong support to public funding programs,[32] observers assume that Republicans are less likely to participate in the checkoff. Similarly, conservatives generally tend to oppose public subsidies and government regulation; thus they are considered less likely to support public financing.

In their 1985 study, Jones and Miller examined the partisanship and ideology of individuals who reported contributing through the checkoff in 1979 and found "somewhat unexpected" patterns. Rank-and-file Republicans were just as likely as Democrats to use the checkoff. Although more than half of those who participated were Democrats, Republican participation was proportionate to their strength in the electorate. The checkoff was also relatively popular among conservatives, although a much greater proportion of liberals than conservatives participated in the checkoff.[33] Whether these patterns have held up since this study was conducted is a matter of speculation, but it is likely that Republican and conservative participation has declined. Unlike the situation in 1979, the program is no longer new, memories of Watergate have dimmed, and participation generally is no longer on the rise. Over the past decade, public financing has become a topic surrounded by fierce partisan debate, and Presidents Reagan and Bush both failed to support the program either in public or in the campaign finance reform packages they submitted to the Congress. To find that partisan biases and ideology still played no significant role in taxpayer decisionmaking would be more "unexpected" today than it was a decade ago.

Given public attitudes, Sorauf surmises that the fact that less than 30 percent of taxpayers contribute through the checkoff "must reflect the belief among some taxpayers—words on the tax return to the contrary—that they increase their tax liability by participating."[34] Many supporters of the program agree with this view or, at least, espouse the related notion that people fail to participate because they do not understand the purpose of the checkoff and the role of public money in the elections process. That taxpayers do misunderstand the law is demonstrated by the results of the 1988 returns, since 17 percent of those who participated were legally ineligible to contribute (see Table 1.4). Other analyses have also documented a lack of public understanding. A 1987 survey of taxpayers in Louisville, Kentucky, found that 19 percent of the respondents were not even aware of the checkoff option. In addition, only 23 percent knew that the funds generated through the checkoff were used to finance general election campaigns and only 40 percent were aware that limits are placed on how much money a candidate may spend.[35] Similar problems have been found in state checkoff programs. A study of the Wisconsin and Minnesota systems, for example, concluded that only 22 percent of those surveyed knew of the state's program and only 65 percent of this group correctly understood the program's tax effect.[36]

In an effort to determine the level of taxpayer understanding and the reasons behind their decisions, the FEC in 1990 initiated a study of public attitudes toward the checkoff program. The Commission retained an independent market research firm to conduct in-depth focus group sessions with diverse gatherings of individuals in Oregon, Tennessee, and New Jersey. In each location, two sessions were held, one with checkoff supporters and the other with nonsupporters. The results shed some light on the problems of the Fund, but provide few clear answers.

The study found that taxpayers know very little about the operation of the public financing program.[37] John Warren McGarry, a member of the Commission, noted that:

> There was not one person in the focus surveys that were conducted across the entire country who understood the Presidential public funding program—not one person. . . . And they had an opportunity to consult with their families and friends. Yet they showed a widespread lack of knowledge and information. Not one could identify the three components of the system or where the checkoff money went.[38]

The taxpayers involved in the focus groups were also confused about the tax implications of the checkoff. About 13 percent of the nonsupporters, for example, misunderstood the tax effects of the checkoff.[39]

The predominant finding of the report, however, was that taxpayers oppose public funding for a broad variety of reasons. Many of these concerns were not specific arguments against public financing per se, but were rooted in broader criticisms of the political system. Participants said they opposed public financing because they disapproved of candidates, the way campaigns are conducted, the electoral system, and government waste. These general attitudes were so pervasive that the authors of the report commented: "It was often difficult to keep the group focused on the subject at hand because of their anger at politicians and a perception of wasteful spending by government. Their anger associated with those concerns contaminated their consideration of Presidential campaign funding and expenditure."[40] The report concluded that "promotional activity" was needed to improve public knowledge, but declared that the "position of nearly all the non-contributors appears to be immovable."[41]

The FEC responded to the study by embarking on a two-year, nationwide public education program. The agency spent $72,000 in 1991 to produce television and radio public service announcements in English and Spanish, which were broadcast during the height of the tax-filing season.[42] These announcements urged taxpayers to make "an informed choice" when deciding whether to designate one dollar of their taxes to the public funding program. The agency also distributed informational flyers, brochures, and editorial pieces, and Commission members made numerous media appearances. In 1992, this public outreach effort was expanded. New public service announcements were produced, and the agency also prepared similar print materials, which were distributed for placement in newspapers and magazines. The agency also distributed information to tax preparers and computer software companies that produce tax preparation packages.

The Commission estimates that its announcements and educational materials reached a potential audience of more than 90 million citizens in 1991 and about 200 million in 1992.[43] It appears, however, to have had little effect: participation did not change appreciably on the 1990 and 1991 tax returns. This education effort, while ambitious, was also relatively modest with respect to both its resources and intensity. A number of national networks and 43 local television stations broadcast the announcement in 1991, although, in most instances, the ad was broadcast infrequently. Nationally, ABC broadcast the ad only five times, CNN two times, and CBS not at all. Many stations ran the announcement no more than two or three times a week for a week or two. Similarly, the radio version of the announcement was aired by a number of national networks and 44 local stations. But the two largest participating networks, NBC/Mutual Radio and Unistar Radio, aired the announcement only twice a week.[44]

This level of exposure was undoubtedly not sufficient to provide taxpayers with a clear understanding of the relatively complex provisions of the public funding program. Nor was it strong enough to outweigh the public perception that the system is not working or the growing feelings of frustration and alienation with the political system. These attitudes are fueled by the barrage of media reports about the failure of the campaign finance regulations, as well as the vocal and persistent criticisms of checkoff opponents. Consequently, the comparatively muted responses of the FEC and supporters of the current system in their attempts to inform the citizenry have not changed public attitudes on a broad scale. Indeed, the primary reason why participation has declined may be the operation of the program itself. Because the system is increasingly perceived as having failed to achieve its goals, an increasingly large share of the public may be losing faith in the system and thus choosing not to participate in the checkoff. To reverse the decline in participation, or at least ensure that taxpayers are making an informed decision, more extensive educational programs than those provided to date will be needed.

Finally, the relatively low level of public awareness and participation is also attributed to the activities of accountants and other tax preparers. In recent years in particular, supporters of the program have charged that accountants fail to inform their clients of the checkoff option, either because of personal opposition or due to a desire to avoid troublesome explanations of political topics. While supporters often cite personal experiences or anecdotes to substantiate this view, there is no solid evidence to verify this claim. The only available data related to this issue comes from the IRS utilization surveys of the 1989 returns, which are noted in Table 1.6. Returns completed by paid preparers, at least for 1988, did show a slightly higher percentage of forms with the boxes left blank and a slightly lower percentage of forms designating a contribution to the checkoff. The difference between these returns and those prepared without the assistance of a preparer, which

TABLE 1.6

CHECKOFF PARTICIPATION BY FORM
OF PREPARATION 1989 RETURNS (%)

	No Preparer	Paid Preparer	Unpaid Preparer	Total
Left Box Blank	11.21	18.84	12.85	14.74
Checked "Yes"	26.91	22.08	25.06	24.67
Checked "No"	61.88	59.08	62.09	60.59
Total	100.00	100.00	100.00	100.00

Note: Based on the IRS Taxpayer Usage Study of selected 1989 returns filed through September 1990.

Source: Federal Election Commission.

is about 4 percent with respect to blank boxes and about 3 percent with respect to "yes" boxes, is not very significant. Certainly, it is not as significant as many have assumed. This difference may fall within the margin of error associated with the IRS sampling procedure. It may also reflect the preparers' understanding of the law. Because tax preparers are presumably more informed about the law, they may make fewer errors in checking the "yes" box when a client has no tax eligibility and instead leave the box blank. The difference may also reflect the diverse characteristics of individuals who complete their own tax forms and those who use a paid or unpaid preparer.

Another common explanation for the lower rate of participation on prepared returns is that the computer software packages used by individual taxpayers and accountants automatically default to "no" and thus encourage nonparticipation. One report claimed that "most of the computer software programs which were used by more than a million taxpayers to prepare their 1990 federal income taxes came from the factory with the presidential campaign fund's $1 checkoff question already answered 'no.'"[45] The FEC has regularly undertaken efforts to explore this concern and monitor computer software packages. In all, the agency has written to 64 manufacturers and received information on nine different programs, and has found that only one package still defaults to "no" if the tax checkoff is not completed. Two other packages also originally defaulted to "no" but were changed in 1991 so that the default option simply leaves the boxes blank. In the other software packages examined by the Commission, the default option leaves the boxes blank. The slight increase in recent years in the number of forms that leave the boxes blank may therefore be a function of the programs used by tax preparers, but the high level of "no" boxes certainly is not.[46]

ASSESSING THE CHECKOFF

For five election cycles, the Presidential Election Campaign Fund has provided more than enough money to finance the costs of presidential campaigns. Yet, taxpayer participation in the program and the amounts designated to the Fund have been on the decline, and Congress has had to restructure the checkoff to avoid the prospect of financial insolvency. Does this prove that the program has failed?

The projected shortfall in Fund revenues was the result of a structural flaw in the law, which adjusts payments to account for inflation without a corresponding adjustment in the amount a taxpayer may contribute. The mechanical application of the law therefore placed the program on an inevitable path toward financial insolvency. If this flaw had been corrected even as late as 1991, the Fund would have been free of financial problems and probably would have had a surplus of more than $140 million after the 1996 election. A decline in taxpayer participation exacerbated the Fund's financial imbalance. This decline, however, was not the major problem. At best, it only served to hasten the advent of a financial crisis by two election cycles.

Changes in the tax structure brought about by recent revisions in the tax code have also had a significant effect on the financial status of the Fund. They have also reduced the number of eligible participants, to a point where at least one out of five taxpayers has been effectively disenfranchised from the system. Those who are eligible are participating less, but the decline is neither as steep or as meaningful as most observers have assumed. While critics contend that the level of participation indicates that a majority of taxpayers have decided that tax dollars should not be used for the financing of campaigns, many of those who choose not to participate do so for reasons other than opposition to public funding. Most importantly, few taxpayers are making an informed choice when completing the checkoff section of their tax forms.

Has the checkoff accomplished its goal? The answer to this question is in part a matter of the perspective of the observer and the assumptions employed in judging support. The primary objective of the checkoff was to broaden participation in the financing of presidential campaigns. The law sought to move away from a system in which a relatively small group of individuals and special interest organizations provided the major portion of campaign war chests to a system wherein a significant portion of a candidate's monies comes from a Fund financed by millions of taxpayers. If one assumes that "broad participation" means that a majority of eligible taxpayers should participate in the program in order for it to qualify as a success, then the current level of participation can be viewed as a sign that the program has not fulfilled its promise. This appears to be the standard by which many critics have come to judge the checkoff. But nowhere in the legislation, in the congressional debates, in the regulations governing the program, or in the administrative rulings issued by the Department of the Treasury and the FEC has majority participation ever been advanced as the criterion for measuring the program's success. In addition, this is the only government program in American history to allow taxpayers to choose whether they want to offer their support. Given the same choice for other government programs, how many would receive the support of even a quarter of eligible taxpayers? A more appropriate measure might be to compare this form of contribution to other methods of political contribution. Such a standard would at least be more in keeping with the general purpose of the law.

When compared to other forms of financial activity, the checkoff has certainly achieved its purpose. Millions of Americans who do not otherwise contribute to political campaigns, organizations, or parties do contribute to the Presidential Election Campaign Fund. In 1980, for example, only 7 percent of voting age citizens donated money to a political candidate and a mere 4 percent gave to a political party, but an estimated 31 percent reported making a contribution through the tax checkoff.[47] Based on a review of these figures, Ruth Jones and Warren Miller concluded that "the implementation of the tax check-off program created a new channel for campaign contributions that more than doubled the number of people making some kind of financial investment in the electoral campaign process in 1980."[48] Similarly, a nationwide University of Michigan study in 1988 found that while 6 percent of the public said they contributed to a candidate and 6 percent said they contributed to a political party during an election year, 27 percent said they made a contribution through the tax checkoff.[49]

Larry Harrington of the Center for Democracy, who supports the checkoff, has tried to place these figures in perspective:

> Almost half of the taxpayers who voted for president in 1988 volunteered for the check-off—almost thirty-three million taxpayers out of sixty-nine million voters. This broad base of funding is remarkable compared to the narrow elitist base of funding in congressional campaigns where, according to a recent study by Citizen Action, one-seventh of one percent of the voting age population contributed forty-nine percent of the money spent by federal candidates.[50]

The percentage of eligible taxpayers who participate in the checkoff is thus much higher than the percentage who give in other ways. Furthermore, it is at least equivalent to the percentage of eligible voters who participate in presidential primaries, while in many states, it is actually higher. Checkoff support is also roughly comparable to the percentage of the electorate that chose to vote in congressional primaries. As Herbert Alexander has written: "The thirty-three million or more persons checking off constitutes a large body of support compared with numbers of those who contribute money, who give service to parties and candidates, or who vote in congressional election years."[51]

So the checkoff has broadened participation. Whether the level of participation achieved justifies the continuance of the program and this form of contribution depends in part on one's perspective, but it clearly has accomplished its goal, although perhaps not so well as some might have hoped. A final assessment of this vehicle also depends on the related question of whether a substantial share of the public will continue to support the program, that is, the question of whether the recent decline in participation will continue. While further promotion of the checkoff will help to answer this question, the answer may ultimately lie in the ability to shore up public confidence in the system. To accomplish this, policymakers will have to address the other major problems that have arisen under the FECA over the past decade.

CHAPTER TWO

FINANCING PRIMARY CAMPAIGNS

R onald Reagan never made a contribution to the Presidential Election Campaign Fund. He was philosophically opposed to the notion of using tax dollars to finance political campaigns. As president, he fought legislation that would have extended public funding to congressional campaigns and, in 1985, his administration proposed a tax package that included a provision to eliminate the income tax checkoff. Yet, in his three bids for his party's presidential nomination, he accepted more than $22.5 million in public matching funds.

Reagan relied heavily on public money in each of his campaigns. His campaign committee emphasized the solicitation of small gifts in order to accumulate matching funds. These subsidies were a significant source of campaign revenue and provided him with a substantial financial advantage over his opponents. In 1976, he received at least $400,000 more in public subsidies than President Gerald Ford. In 1980, he received $1.6 million more than his nearest challenger, George Bush. In 1984, as the incumbent president, Reagan essentially ran without opposition, but his campaign nevertheless accepted $10.1 million in matching funds, which was the maximum amount allowed by the law. No other candidate has qualified for the maximum subsidy in the five primary elections conducted under the public funding program.

To receive these funds, Reagan had to agree to follow the campaign spending limits established by the FECA. These limits, however, were easily circumvented. One of the ways Reagan avoided the law was by establishing a political action committee (PAC) before becoming a candidate and using it as a shadow campaign committee. This

committee proved to be an effective vehicle for avoiding the spending ceilings. The PAC conducted a wide range of campaign-related
activities prior to the 1980 and 1984 elections, but none of its expenditures were subject to the campaign spending ceilings because they
failed to meet the legal definitions used to determine whether an expenditure is an actual campaign expense. In addition, Reagan's campaign
committees also circumvented the spending caps by taking advantage of technical provisions in the law to spend more than allowed
in state contests. Even with these actions, however, FEC audits determined that Reagan violated the spending law in New Hampshire in
both 1976 and 1980. But the Commission's decisions did not affect
Reagan's chances in either race, for they were rendered years after the
voting had taken place.

Reagan's experience epitomizes the experience with public financing in presidential primary campaigns. On the one hand, the matching
funds program has proven to be an extremely popular form of campaign
finance and an important source of revenue. It has been widely accepted by candidates and has encouraged them to solicit small contributions
instead of large gifts and PAC donations. The program has been especially helpful to lesser-known aspirants who lack broad bases of financial support and to candidates who lack ready access to substantial
numbers of large donors. By providing such candidates with the funds
needed to introduce themselves to voters, public funding has increased
the choices available to the electorate and enhanced the competitiveness of nomination contests.

On the other hand, the expenditure ceilings that accompany the
acceptance of public money have been roundly criticized as little more
than parchment barriers. Many critics, as well as some supporters, argue
that the primary effect of these restraints has been to induce candidates
to find ways to circumvent the law. Candidates have responded to the
new rules by retaining lawyers and accountants well-versed in the
nuances of the regulations, whose task is to find innovative methods of
avoiding the restrictions placed on contributions and spending. These
practitioners have had few problems finding ways to evade the law. As
a result, the ceilings have become so porous that they have had little pos-
itive effect on spending. Moreover, the FEC has generally failed to take
actions that would strengthen the limits or deter further subversions, which
has encouraged even bolder efforts in defiance of the law.

The primary purpose behind the creation of the public subsidies program was to provide candidates with an alternative source of funding in
order to diminish the role of special interests in the political process. By
linking public grants to small contributions, Congress also sought to eliminate the reliance on large contributions that had become a commonplace

feature of presidential campaigns. The program was also designed to enhance electoral competition by providing candidates with the revenue needed to communicate with voters and by establishing spending limits to guard against the possibility of a candidate gaining victory simply by out-spending all opponents. How well these objectives have been achieved is a subject of much controversy.

MONEY WITHOUT INTEREST

Since 1976, the public matching funds program has provided more than $200 million to 61 candidates. Every serious major party candidate has participated in the program with the exception of Republican John Connally in 1980. Connally apparently chose not to participate due to his concerns with the spending limit. He perceived that the only way he could compete with Reagan was to spend more than the limit in those states where he felt he had a chance of winning. His decision to reject the subsidy should, therefore, not be taken as an objection to public funding itself.[1]

The distribution of matching funds shows no partisan preference. Overall, 37 Democrats have received approximately $105.7 million in matching funds and 17 Republicans have received about $91.9 million (see Table 2.1).[2] That more Democrats have received public funds is simply a matter of the greater number of open races for the Democratic presidential nomination

TABLE 2.1

SUMMARY OF MATCHING FUNDS PAYMENTS, 1976–1992

Year	Democrats		Republicans		Others[a]	
	Number of Candidates	Amount ($ millions)	Number of Candidates	Amount ($ millions)	Number of Candidates	Amount ($ millions)
1992	7	24.63	2	15.86	2	2.37
1988	7	30.29	6	35.49	2	1.76
1984	8	25.73	1	10.10	1	0.69
1980	3	10.14	6	20.76	1	0.53
1976	12	14.95	2	9.75	1	0.25
Total	37	105.74	17	91.96	7	5.60

[a] These totals include Ellen McCormack, the anti-abortion candidate who ran as a Democrat in 1976, and Lyndon LaRouche, who ran as a Democrat in 1980, 1984, and 1988.

Source: Federal Election Commission.

during this period and the large number of candidates that have chosen to run in these years. In the two elections in which the Republicans had an open race, they have received the largest share of public funds. This includes 1988, an election in which neither party had an incumbent seeking the nomination, when the Republicans, despite a smaller number of candidates, received about $35.5 million in taxpayers' funds compared to $30.3 million for the Democrats.

Republicans, on average, have actually fared much better under the program than have their potential opponents. The average amount received by Republican challengers is $5.41 million, as compared to $2.86 million for the Democrats. In addition, the top three recipients of matching subsidies to date are all Republicans. George Bush leads the list, having amassed more than $24.7 million in public grants in his three bids for his party's nomination. He is followed closely by Reagan, who took in more than $22.5 million in his three runs, while further behind is Marion "Pat" Robertson, who in 1988 alone raised more than $10.4 million in matching monies. The top Democrat is Walter Mondale, who received about $9.5 million from the government in his 1984 campaign. He is followed closely by Democrat Michael Dukakis, who raised about $9 million in matching funds in 1988.[3]

Matching funds have therefore been an important source of revenue for presidential candidates. Just how important is indicated by the figures in Table 2.2. In each election since 1976, approximately a third of the monies raised by all candidates came from public subsidies. This percentage is even higher for those candidates who placed greater reliance on subsidies. These individuals usually received at least 40 percent of their campaign funds from the matching program.[4] Others, especially those who pursued larger contributions, tended to receive a lower portion of their funds in public monies. Yet, even for these individuals, public funds usually constituted at least 25 to 30 percent of their total receipts. The lone exception to this general rule is Lyndon LaRouche, the extremist candidate who qualified for matching funds in each of the elections of the 1980s. In each of these elections, he had the lowest percentage of total revenues from matching funds and, in 1984, his percentage was an unusually low 11 percent. If he is excluded from consideration, the minimum share for any candidate in each of the past four elections is a surprisingly stable 27 percent.[5]

What is most notable about this dependence on matching funds is how remarkably consistent it has been. Despite the diversity of candidates who have sought the nomination, the different political circumstances that have surrounded each election, the development of new and more sophisticated fundraising techniques, and the rising costs of campaigns, the overall percentage of revenues raised through matching funds has varied very little. This indicates the program's enduring popularity with

TABLE 2.2

PERCENT OF PRIMARY RECEIPTS FROM MATCHING FUNDS, 1976–1992

	1976	1980	1984	1988	1992
Highest % Received by a Candidate	46	40	46	44	47
Lowest % Received by a Candidate	30	25	11	21	27
Lowest % Received by a Candidate (excluding LaRouche)	30	27	26	26	27
Overall % All Candidates	36	33	33	31	34

Note: Based on the adjusted receipts reported by all candidates that qualified for public funding as of May 1993.

Source: Federal Election Commission.

candidates and its continuing importance as a source of campaign money. It also indicates one of the primary benefits of the public funding program—that it allows candidates seeking their party's nomination to pursue diverse fundraising strategies.

The public funding option opens the door to a number of effective fundraising approaches. Candidates do not have to rely on their success in soliciting large contributions in order to be financially competitive or raise the sums needed to finance a viable campaign. They can design their fundraising strategies to conform to their political strengths and to maximize the revenue potential of their base of support. Candidates without access to large donors or those with broad bases of support can focus on the solicitation of small, matchable contributions to double the revenue produced by their fundraising efforts. Candidates with access to large donors can focus on the solicitation of larger individual gifts of up to $1,000. By doing so, they can raise money more efficiently, amass large sums relatively quickly, and still earn matching funds on the first $250 contributed by each individual. Others may choose a more differentiated approach that taps both small and large donors.

In recent elections, each of these alternative approaches has been used effectively by candidates in both parties to raise the monies needed to finance their campaigns. The range of possible options was most clearly displayed in 1992. President Bush entered the race with perhaps the most well-established financial base in recent electoral history. He had essentially spent 12 years developing financial support, first as a candidate, then as vice president, and finally as president. In his 1988 bid for the Republican nomination, he adopted a fundraising approach designed to exploit his ability to attract large donations. He raised the maximum amount allowed under the law, more than $27 million, $16.5 million of which came from $1,000 contributions.[6] In 1992, he pursued a similar strategy. Almost 83 percent of the amount he raised from private contributions, about $22.4 million, was received in contributions of $500 or more. Only 15 percent came from small contributions of $200 or less. Despite this emphasis on large gifts, Bush still received a sizeable public subsidy: overall, 27 percent of his total revenues came from matching funds.[7]

Bush's opponent, former Nixon speech writer and conservative political commentator Patrick Buchanan, lacked a comparable fundraising base and therefore adopted a different approach. His campaign emphasized the solicitation of small contributions through direct mail and the accumulation of matching funds. Only 13 percent of the funds Buchanan raised privately came from contributions of $500 or more. The vast majority of his revenues, more than 76 percent, was received in contributions of $200 or less, and 38 percent of his total revenues came from matching funds. Democrat Jerry Brown, Buchanan's polar opposite ideologically, pursued a similar, albeit more radical, version of this approach. Brown based his fundraising solely on small contributions and the corresponding public grants. He framed his fundraising strategy to reflect his platform of political reform by refusing to accept any contribution of more than $100. Accordingly, all of his funds, with the exception of some loans his campaign received in anticipation of matching fund payments, came from small donations and 45 percent of his total revenues came from public subsidies.[8]

Democrats Bill Clinton, the party's eventual nominee, and former Senator Paul Tsongas employed more varied approaches. Their fundraising strategies were designed to produce more of a balance between large and small donations. Clinton raised about 45 percent of the funds he received from private sources in contributions of $500 or more, and close to 42 percent in contributions of $200 or less. Approximately 33 percent of his total revenue came from public monies. Tsongas raised about 40 percent of his funds from private sources in contributions of $500 or more, and about 43 percent in contributions of $200 or less. Approximately 36 percent of his total revenues came from public monies.

Similar patterns are found in other elections. For example, in 1988, the Reverend Jesse Jackson, a Democrat, and Pat Robertson, a Republican, adopted strategies along the lines of Buchanan's approach. Republicans Robert Dole and Jack Kemp, as well as Democrat Michael Dukakis, employed the more varied approach used by Clinton and Tsongas in 1992. The matching funds program has thus benefited candidates in both parties. Moreover, there is no clear pattern characteristic of one party or the other. Democrats do not necessarily rely on public subsidies more heavily than Republicans, nor do Republicans necessarily rely on large donors to a greater extent than Democrats.

If any group could be isolated as the "primary beneficiaries" of the matching funds program, it would probably be the lesser-known aspirants who enter the presidential sweepstakes without a broad base of large donors. For these individuals, public subsidies have proven to be a source of sorely needed revenue. The grants have helped to ensure that these candidates have the funds needed to communicate their ideas to voters. Public financing has therefore provided these candidates with an opportunity to run for president and thus enhanced the choices available to the electorate. It has also, in turn, improved the competitiveness of nomination contests. This aspect of the program has been noted by Herbert Alexander, director of the Citizens' Research Foundation and the nation's leading expert on the presidential campaign finance system.

> The most positive aspect of public financing has been the opportunity it has given certain candidates to compete in the political system. Since the presidential matching system was first employed in 1976, matching funds have provided potential candidates who lacked name recognition or access to large amounts of private campaign funds the opportunity to effectively contend for presidential nomination. If it were not for the combination of contribution limits and public funding, Jimmy Carter, who lacked access to traditional sources of large Democratic contributions, probably would have lost out early in the 1976 primary season to those candidates such as Senator Henry M. Jackson, who enjoyed such access. In 1980 public funds helped George Bush establish himself as Ronald Reagan's major competitor. . . . In 1984 matching funds helped Senator Gary Hart refill his depleted campaign treasury following his unexpected New Hampshire primary victory and the subsequent upsurge in contributions helped carry his campaign to the convention. . . . Matching funds helped keep Jesse Jackson's underfinanced but nevertheless well-publicized campaigns competitive in both 1984 and 1988. In all these cases the matching funds provisions of the F.E.C.A. [sic]

opened up the electoral process to some candidates
whose campaign otherwise might not have been able to
survive. [9]

This list might be expanded to include Bill Clinton, who emerged as the
early frontrunner in a field of relatively unknown Democrats in part as
a result of his fundraising lead, which included a matching funds advantage of close to a million dollars over his chief rival, Paul Tsongas.[10] The
matching funds he accumulated prior to the New Hampshire primary
then helped to finance his Super Tuesday success and the crucial victory
in the Illinois primary that helped secure the nomination.

To say that public funding has improved competition is not to say
that well-known candidates have been unduly disadvantaged by the program. These candidates also benefit from public financing because they
usually have much broader bases of political support than their less prominent challengers. By soliciting small contributions from their supporters, well-known candidates can usually generate thousands of matchable
donations, which yield substantial amounts of matching revenue. The
law thus encourages even the best-known contenders to solicit small donations. Those who do are certain to enjoy a substantial resource advantage over their opponents.

This is especially true in the earliest stages of a presidential race. Because
the first matching payment is not issued by the Treasury until January
1 of the election year, well-known candidates who enter the race with
public name recognition and a broad base of potential support can capitalize on these advantages by emphasizing the solicitation of matchable
contributions. By doing so, they can gain a significant fundraising advantage in the critical period just prior to the Iowa caucus and New Hampshire
primary. For example, in 1984, Democrat Walter Mondale adopted this
approach and gained a sizeable financial windfall when the first subsidy
checks were issued. His first matching fund payment was about $4.3 mil-
lion, or about $2 million more than that of his closest rival, John Glenn,
who received around $2.3 million.[11] In 1988, George Bush had amassed
over $6.1 million in matching funds by the time of the first payment, which
was slightly less than a million dollars more than the amount raised by
his chief rival, Senator Robert Dole, but was close to $3 million more than
the amount earned by Representative Jack Kemp and more than $4 mil-
lion over the amount earned by Pierre "Pete" du Pont.[12]

The public funding program has thus achieved its principal objective.
It has provided candidates with an alternative source of revenue and
encouraged them to finance their campaigns with small contributions. The
program has thus helped to broaden financial participation in the presidential selection process. At the same time, it has served to diminish the

role of special interest money in presidential campaigns. Because PAC contributions are not eligible for matching funds, candidates can raise more money by soliciting small contributions than PAC contributions. If a candidate solicits $5,000 in small contributions, the total amount of revenue generated is $10,000 because of the matching funds. A PAC contribution of $5,000 merely produces $5,000 in revenue. The law thus gives candidates a strong incentive to choose small private gifts over PAC money. This incentive, as well as the practice of many PACs to forego making contributions in processes that select major party candidates,[13] have led to a system in which PAC contributions play an insignificant role. On average, only two to four percent of the total monies raised by presidential aspirants comes from PACs, as compared to congressional campaigns, which often rely on PACs for 30 to 40 percent of their total revenue.

FINANCING MINOR CANDIDATES

A number of minor party candidates have also benefited from the public funding program. In 1984, Sonia Johnson of the Citizens party became the first such candidate to qualify for matching funds and she received about $193,000. Since then, two other minor party challengers have met the requirements of the program. Lenora Fulani of the New Alliance party earned slightly less than a million dollars in 1988 and about $2 million in 1992. John Hagelin of the Natural Law party also earned matching funds in the most recent election, raising about $350,000. In addition, Lyndon LaRouche, a minor candidate who ran as a Democrat in each of the elections during the 1980s, earned a total of $1.8 million in matching funds over the course of three elections. Minor candidates have thus received about $5.3 million, or less than three percent of the total amount that has been distributed through the program.

While the monies given to minor party candidates are relatively insignificant when compared to the sums received by major party contenders, the financing of minor candidates has become a matter of some controversy. Supporters argue that this experience demonstrates the value of the program since it has provided funds to candidates regardless of party affiliation and has thus provided funds to candidates who have traditionally fared poorly in a system based solely on private monies. Public funding has thus improved the ability of minor candidates to communicate with voters and has expanded the options available to the electorate. Critics place more emphasis on the fact that taxpayers' dollars are being given to candidates who are not supported by the vast majority of citizens. Instead of reflecting voter preferences, the program is simply serving to promote "fringe" candidates, which has further undermined public support of the campaign finance system.

Some minor parties have found it easy to qualify for public sub-sidies because the eligibility criteria are rather lenient. The basic eligi-bility requirement, raising $5,000 in small contributions in 20 states, has not been revised since the matching program was adopted in 1974. In theory, this requirement should prove less burdensome with each new election cycle since the real value of the financial threshold decreases. The $5,000 established in 1974 is comparable to less than $2,000 now. What is interesting is that despite the relative easing of this bur-den, only a few of the dozens of minor parties that might seek public funding have qualified for the subsidies. It appears that the threshold still poses some barrier for minor candidates, but a tougher qualifying threshold would help to ensure that those who do receive funds have a broad base of support.

More important than the qualifying threshold have been the rules adopted by the FEC in administering the program. The Commission has had to face a number of questions regarding candidate eligibility for match-ing funds and it has consistently pursued an approach that operates on the side of leniency and the promotion of candidate participation. For example, the 1976 amendments to the FECA contained a provision that called for the termination of a candidate's eligibility within 30 days if that candidate received less than 10 percent of the vote in consecu-tive primaries.[14] This provision was adopted to "separate serious candi-dates from those who are not going to be nominated" by ensuring that candidates did not stay in the race simply because they had access to pub-lic funds.[15] A minor party candidate, however, frequently becomes the party's presidential nominee without opposition. The FEC has therefore decided that the 10 percent rule does not apply in these instances and that the candidate is eligible to receive public subsidies until the party's convention or until the time of the last major party nominating con-vention. Consequently, a minor party candidate may remain eligible for public money well after the time when a major party candidate has been declared ineligible.

The effect of the ten percent rule has been further diminished by FEC regulations that allow a candidate to exclude particular primaries from this requirement.[16] In this way, a candidate can continue to be eligible for matching funds despite a poor showing in a number of primaries. For example, in 1992, New Alliance party candidate Lenora Fulani informed the Commission that she would seek the nomination under the banner of a number of different parties in a selected number of states.[17] She thus remained eligible for funding despite poor showings in the initial primaries. The Commission also allows candidates to qualify for matching funds after failing to capture 10 percent of the vote in a number of primaries. This is how John Hagelin of the Natural Law party and Democrat Larry

Agran became eligible for funding in 1992. These candidates did not reach the qualifying threshold until well after the primaries had begun. Agran did not become eligible for matching funds until mid-May and ended up receiving about $270,000.[18] Hagelin did not become eligible until October 15, three weeks before the general election, but because the Natural Law party's nominating convention was not held until early October, the FEC recognized his submission and awarded him a matching payment of about $350,000.[19]

In addressing the issue of minor candidate eligibility, the FEC has had to balance a number of legitimate interests. Minor party financing thus illustrates some of the conflicting policy demands the Commission must confront in attempting to carry out the law. As the agency responsible for certifying matching payments, the FEC is cast in the role of "guardian of the public purse" and must ensure that taxpayer money is used in accordance with the law. Those who criticize the subsidizing of "fringe" candidates tend to emphasize this aspect of the Commission's work and further note that in fulfilling this role the agency funds candidates who enjoy little public support. The law acknowledges this concern by stopping payments to candidates who fail to demonstrate a minimal level of support in consecutive primaries. But the agency is also responsible for encouraging participation in the political process and enhancing electoral choice since these are two of the purposes the campaign finance laws seek to achieve. A much stricter interpretation of the law might severely reduce the funds available to candidates and serve to discourage participation.

The FEC has also tried to recognize the principle that candidates should have some choice in deciding how to conduct their campaigns and the right of party organizations to determine the methods used to decide their presidential nomination. There are different types of candidates and different ways to seek a party's nomination, and the FEC has taken an approach that attempts to minimize the effect of the regulations in restricting candidate options. By allowing candidates to decide where they want to compete, the agency has not only helped minor party candidates but has also recognized the reality that a candidate does not have to run everywhere in order to contest the nomination. If the Commission adopted a more stringent standard, it would penalize not only minor candidates, but also "favorite son" challengers or major party candidates who adopt a regional strategy based on performing well in selected states. A stricter approach might also exclude major party candidates who fail to qualify for delegates in some states, such as Gary Hart in 1984.

The current approach thus promotes some of the central goals of the public financing system. It also guards against an overly burdensome regulatory approach that might reduce participation or restrict legitimate candidate strategies. While some may be concerned that the law has become

too lenient, others feel that minor party candidates deserve an opportunity to present their views and public funding has provided it. The FEC
has taken a reasonable approach on this issue: it administers the law fairly and leaves it to the voters to decide whom to support.

THE CONFLICTING PRESSURES OF THE FECA

While the reforms of the 1970s have assisted with the financing of
campaigns, they have also increased the financial pressures on candidates. The contribution limits of the FECA require candidates to finance
their campaigns through individual contributions of $1,000 or less,
and the public funding program encourages the solicitation of smaller
gifts. Given these parameters, candidates must develop a broad base of
financial support and raise tens of thousands of contributions if they are
to raise the sums needed to mount a viable national campaign. This is
a burdensome and time-consuming task, especially for challengers who
enter the race with a limited base of financial support. Candidates
therefore need to begin raising money long before the first votes are cast
in the presidential selection process.

The public funding program also promotes early fundraising because
of the timetable it establishes for eligible donations. Any contribution
made or received after January 1 of the year before the election is eligible for matching. This provision allows candidates to begin soliciting matchable donations as early in the preelection year as possible. Candidates
who do begin raising funds early, and do so successfully, normally
receive a sizeable sum when the first matching payments are issued at
the beginning of the election year. Lesser-known challengers thus have
an incentive to start campaigning early because the matching funds they
earn in the preelection year can provide them with the funds needed to
be perceived as credible candidates or to be able to compete in the crucial early stages of the primary season. Well-known contenders have an
incentive to start early because they can capitalize on their established
donor base and name recognition to achieve a substantial financial
advantage over their opponents.

This pressure to begin raising funds early intensified throughout the
1980s due to the operational effects of the spending limits. Under the
provisions of the FECA, the spending limits are adjusted for inflation but
the contribution limits are not. The amount a candidate may spend in
seeking the nomination has therefore increased from the original $12
million ($10 million plus 20 percent for fundraising expenses) established
in 1974 to more than $33 million in 1992. The maximum amount an
individual can give to a candidate, however, is set at $1,000. Consequently,
in each succeeding election, candidates must devote more time to

fundraising and generate an increasingly large number of contributions in order to raise the sum permitted under the spending limit. This encourages candidates to begin raising money earlier and earlier with each new election cycle.

Changes in the presidential selection process have also helped to encourage early campaigning. Throughout the 1980s, the primary calendar became increasingly "front-loaded" as an increasing number of states decided to hold their elections during the six-week period between mid-February and the end of March. In addition, a number of states shifted from more party-oriented caucuses to more open primary elections as their means of selecting a candidate and choosing convention delegates. These decisions dramatically increased the financial demands of the initial weeks of the formal selection process.[20] Candidates must now stage campaigns in a number of states simultaneously and conduct expensive media campaigns, sometimes beginning as early as January, to attract the wide support needed to win primary contests. They must therefore amass large sums of money prior to the middle of February if they are to be assured of having the resources needed to wage an effective campaign.

The campaign finance laws and changes in the nomination process have thus combined to force candidates to begin campaigning early. In most cases, candidates start to raise funds a year or more before the initial contests in Iowa and New Hampshire in an effort to amass the funds needed to wage a viable national campaign. Those who fail to start early risk the prospect of facing challengers who enjoy a significant financial advantage in the initial contests that play a crucial role in shaping public perceptions of the race.

The only election that has not followed this pattern, of course, is the 1992 race. Only one candidate, Paul Tsongas, began to campaign early in the preelection year. His opponents all waited until late August and thereafter to declare their intentions. This late start, however, was a result of the unique political situation in 1991. It did not reflect any change in the effects of the law or in the decisions made by challengers as to the best way to launch a presidential bid. President Bush's historic level of popularity in the wake of the Gulf War and the decision by all of the putative Democratic frontrunners to forego a race against an incumbent who was perceived to be unbeatable created a situation in which the Democratic race got off to a very delayed start. It also left the race open to a number of relatively unknown challengers, who decided to enter the race as it became clear that many of their more established partisans had chosen not to run. In 1996, it is highly unlikely that a similar situation will exist. Instead, 1996, at least on the Republican side, will probably be very similar to the Democratic nomination in 1984 or the race in both parties in 1988. In a competitive contest of this sort, candidates will have to start early to amass the substantial war chest needed to finance the first stage of the primaries.

The late start in 1992, however, is also the exception that tends to support the rule. Because the Democratic aspirants did not enter the race with well-established fundraising bases, as did President Bush, and did not begin to campaign early, they had to devote an inordinate amount of time to fundraising. By November 1991, only four months before the New Hampshire primary, most of the Democrats were spending at least half of their time raising money.[21] Even so, all of these campaigns were relatively under-financed in comparison to previous contests. For example, by the end of January, Bill Clinton had raised about $5.4 million, which was almost $2 million more than his nearest challenger. In 1988, Clinton would have been fifth in the fundraising rankings with this amount, or more than $9 million behind Michael Dukakis.[22] By mid-February, most of the Democrats had to secure loans against anticipated matching fund receipts to help finance their campaigns. After New Hampshire, they were all struggling financially because they lacked the reserves needed to cover the heavy expenditures that accompanied the numerous state elections in the first ten days of March. As a result, the three candidates who remained in the race, Clinton, Tsongas, and Brown, could manage to wage full-fledged campaigns in only a handful of states. Since they did not have an opportunity to develop a fundraising base during the year before the election, the candidates had to spend an extensive amount of time throughout the campaign raising the monies needed to maintain their efforts.

These pressures to begin campaigning early would not be of great concern to candidates were it not for the spending limits.[23] Without these ceilings, candidates could simply adapt to the strategic and operational demands of the reforms by beginning their campaigns early enough to accommodate them. But this option is not readily available in a system that limits the amount a candidate may spend. The FECA's limits on state-by-state and aggregate expenditures are designed to induce candidates to restrict the lengths of their campaigns and their level of early campaigning. Candidates who begin to campaign far in advance of the first contests and spend substantial amounts in the preelection year run the risk of having to curtail their campaigning during the election year in order to comply with the limits. No candidate wants to face this possibility. Instead, challengers, especially potential frontrunners, want to limit early spending in order to maximize the amounts they can spend in state primaries and caucuses. One of the largely unexpected outcomes of the law is thus that it has presented candidates with a central strategic problem: how to accomplish the early campaigning required by the finance laws without violating the campaign spending limits.

Candidates have been especially concerned with the spending limits because it is impossible to predict with any precision the overall resource demands of a campaign, the amount that should be spent in the pre-election year to accomplish a campaign's strategic and organizational objectives, and the outcome of state delegate selection contests. It is therefore difficult to determine in advance whether a campaign will reach the limit in a particular state or approach the aggregate national ceiling. Every campaign must therefore consider the potential effects of the limits when making strategic and organizational decisions.

This concern with the limits was probably envisioned by the authors of the FECA. After all, the basic purpose of spending restraints is to force candidates to make decisions that will control the costs of campaigns and make judgments about how to allocate funds in a context of limited resources. This intent is reflected in the vast difference between the state ceilings and the aggregate limit. In 1992, the sum of the state ceilings was more than $86 million, but a candidate could spend no more than $33 million. Candidates therefore have to decide how to allocate their expenditures between states in order to achieve their political objectives, the most important of which are to win state elections and a majority of the convention delegates, and yet remain within the overall cap.

The resource decisions prompted by the spending limits are particularly troublesome for candidates and their staffs because these ceilings fail to reflect the realities of presidential campaigns. While the law allows an additional 20 percent in expenditures to defray fundraising costs, the actual costs of raising money are often greater than 20 cents on the dollar.[24] Although the ceilings are adjusted for increases in the Consumer Price Index, the real costs of such campaign staples as postage and air travel, not to mention the new campaign technologies such as polling, television advertising, computerized mail services, and satellite transmissions, have increased at rates much higher than that of inflation. As FEC Commissioner Lee Ann Elliott has noted, "In truth, campaign costs don't go up at marketbasket inflation; instead of going up about four or five percent every year, they go up *ten, twelve, fifteen* percent every year."[25] Finally, since the state spending limits are based on population, they also fail to reflect the enhanced revenue demands of the reformed selection process or the relative importance of different state contests. Iowa, the nation's first and most important caucus state, has a lower ceiling than those established in more than half of the states. New Hampshire, the nation's most important primary state, has the lowest state spending limit—candidates may only spend the minimum amount allowed for any state in this crucial contest.

The ceilings have induced some candidates to restrict their spending. In the first four elections conducted under the FECA, at least five candidates had to cut back significantly on their anticipated spending or were reluctant to spend available funds because of the aggregate limit: Ford and Reagan in 1976, Reagan in 1980, Mondale in 1984, and Bush in 1988.[26] The predominant response to the law, however, has not been to reduce spending or ensure tight-fisted control over the allocation of resources. Rather, candidates have responded to the law by following the compelling logic of their new strategic environment and seeking ways to circumvent the limits. The limits have, as Herbert Alexander and Monica Bauer have written, "forced candidates to engage in subterfuges that make a mockery of the law and further confuse the funding picture."[27]

CIRCUMVENTING THE LIMITS

The penalties for exceeding the spending limits are not unduly severe. Since 1984, the FEC requires that a candidate simply repay to the Treasury an amount equal to the percentage of excess spending that represents public funds. This percentage is usually around 33 percent, which results in a repayment of about one dollar for every three in excess spending. Most candidates would consider this a bargain, particularly since no fine is assessed until the FEC completes its audit of a campaign, which normally occurs more than a year after the voting has taken place.

With such a low penalty, why have candidates been so concerned about breaking the law? The reason is that they fear the potential political consequences of violating the limits. Press reports announcing that a candidate "had broken the law" might raise questions about a candidate's integrity and cast a shadow over his or her campaign. Opponents may attempt to exploit such stories and make them an issue in the campaign, thus forcing the offender to spend time and money countering these charges. Even if a campaign has not exceeded the limit in a state, heavy early spending could place a candidate in a vulnerable strategic position. Such a candidate might have to face a situation in which he or she can be outspent by less extravagant opponents in the final weeks of a particular state contest and thereby suffer a defeat or win by a smaller margin than expected, which may lead to speculation about the candidate's "weakness." Another concern is that the spending limit will become an issue in the press and lead to speculation that a candidate is "in trouble" because he or she can not spend as freely as other competitors.

These sorts of considerations have induced candidates to find ways to minimize the expenditures they need to report under the spending ceilings. This has been especially true for the states of Iowa and New Hampshire. These states play such an important role in the presidential selection process that candidates feel compelled to spend as much as possible in these contests. As a result, these two states are the only states in which candidates are likely to exceed the spending limit. To avoid this outcome, candidates have adopted a wide range of what could almost be cast as "standard operating procedures" that have completely undermined the efficacy of the law.

The most common evasion employed by candidates is to take advantage of the valid exemptions contained in the law. The FECA regulations were designed to reflect the realities of presidential campaigns insofar as they recognize that certain types of spending, if counted against state limits, could place a candidate at a strategic disadvantage or undermine a contender's ability to wage an effective campaign. The rules allow candidates to allocate certain fundraising costs incurred within a state to the overall fundraising limit instead of the state ceiling. They exempt the lodging and travel costs of candidates and their traveling staffs if they are in a state for only a few days so as not to discourage personal campaigning and thus deny voters a chance to meet those running. Costs of complying with the law are also exempted to help ensure implementation of the law and effective reporting. Finally, the law allows candidates to apportion media expenses based on their potential statewide audience. So, for example, in 1992, candidates buying media time on Boston television stations only had to allocate about 16 percent of their expenditures against the New Hampshire limit, since only 16 percent of the Boston market consists of New Hampshire viewers.[28]

Campaign lawyers and accountants have exploited these provisions by developing innovative allocation schemes and creative accounting systems for apportioning state expenses. They have applied the fundraising and compliance exemptions to as many types of expenditures as possible. They have housed campaign staff just over state borders or asked them to sleep out-of-state every fourth night. More importantly, they have taken the allocation principle used for media expenditures and applied it to all sorts of activities. For example, they have established "regional headquarters" to defray the cost of overhead and administrative expenses in a particular state; hired out-of-state phone banks that supposedly canvass in more than one state; interviewed persons in other states to defray the cost of a statewide poll; and shifted as many costs as possible to their national headquarters. These tactics, which for the most part represent the tip of the iceberg with respect to the evasive schemes candidates employ, have allowed candidates to spend hundreds of thousands of dollars more than the amounts permitted in Iowa and New Hampshire. They have also forced the FEC auditors into the position of having to confront constantly changing practices that they are asked to unravel and judge.

Another subversive practice that became increasingly common among prospective candidates during the 1980s was the establishment of a precandidacy PAC or some other organizational vehicle to conduct financial activities outside of the parameters of the law. This approach was first used by Ronald Reagan, who established a PAC in 1977 as a means of disposing of $1.6 million in surplus funds from his 1976 campaign. The original purpose of this committee was to provide assistance to conservative Republican candidates and causes. Reagan and his advisers soon discovered that this committee could serve a dual purpose, since it could also be used to conduct a wide range of campaign-related activities that would keep Reagan in the public spotlight and allow him to expand his political organization in preparation for a possible run in 1980. This insight became the PAC's operative principle and, over the next three years, the committee raised close to $5 million, most of which was used to hire a staff, finance a political operation, recruit volunteers, and subsidize Reagan's travel.[29]

None of the monies raised or spent by Reagan's group were subject to the contribution and spending limits imposed on presidential campaigns. Under the guidelines established by the FECA, any individual or group, even a prospective presidential candidate, may legally form a PAC. Even if the future candidate is the head of the PAC, this type of committee is considered to be independent of any future campaign committee, so long as the PAC and its members avoid a handful of very specific activities that are used by the FEC to decide whether an individual should be regarded as a candidate subject to the law. These activities include the staging of media campaigns to announce the potential candidate's intention to seek the nomination, using PAC money to qualify the future candidate for state ballots, and presenting an individual as a future candidate in PAC publications. These actions are so narrowly defined that they are easily avoided. Accordingly, none of the monies raised or spent by Reagan's committee were applied to the contribution and spending limits governing the 1980 campaign.

Given the advantages of a PAC, it is not surprising that an increasing number of presidential aspirants established these committees during the 1980s. Prior to the 1980 election, three of Reagan's fellow Republicans formed PACs of their own in an effort to keep pace with his efforts. In advance of the 1984 contest, five candidates formed committees as four Democratic challengers joined Reagan in adopting this organizational approach. By 1988, this tactic had become a common feature of presidential electoral politics, with ten of thirteen major party candidates setting up PACs prior to declaring their candidacies.[30] The amounts spent by these committees rose even more dramatically, growing from $7.48 million in the 1980 cycle to more than $25.2 million in 1988. In all, this use of these committees led to more than $40 million in expenditures outside of the spending limits.

Even with these schemes and machinations, candidates have still exceeded the spending limits. In almost every instance, however, the overspending occurred in only two states—Iowa and New Hampshire (see Table 2.3). The ceilings are essentially meaningless in every other state. In fact, the only other state to have its limit exceeded is Maine, another early contest, and this ceiling was breached by only one candidate in 1980 and another in 1984. Only three of the more than 50 different candidates who have received public money have surpassed the overall ceiling on expenditures: Mondale spent about $579,000 more than allowed in 1984, Bush spent about $214,000 more in 1988 and Robertson spent about $660,000 more in 1988. In each of these instances, the offender spent less than two-and-one-half percent more than the limit permitted.

Not only have an increasing number of candidates violated the Iowa and New Hampshire limits, but they have also exceeded these limits by increasingly large amounts. In 1980, for example, three candidates exceeded the New Hampshire limit by an average amount of $31,400. In 1988, six candidates violated the New Hampshire limit by an average amount of $219,000. Moreover, in most instances, overspending in one of these two states represented the majority of the repayment a candidate was required to make and, in four instances, it was the only infraction for which a candidate was fined.

This last point highlights another problem with the state spending limits: they force FEC auditors to spend an enormous amount of time investigating state expenditures. The Commission's audit division has been severely criticized for the long time it takes to complete its review of a presidential campaign.[31] Part of the reason for this delay is a lack of adequate staffing,[32] but it is also due to the complex nature of the transactions used to avoid the spending limits. The FEC estimates that the monitoring of these ceilings has comprised roughly 50 percent of the time spent in auditing presidential campaigns.[33] In the view of former FEC Chair John Warren McGarry, the limits have become "a major impediment to the swift completion of campaign audits."[34]

Following the 1988 election, the FEC admitted that the experiment with state spending limits had failed. The agency noted that "the limitations have had little impact on campaign spending in a given state" and have "proven a significant accounting burden for campaigns and an equally difficult audit and enforcement task."[35] Accordingly, in 1990 and 1991, the Commission revised its rules to simplify the process of allocating expenses to state ceilings. Beginning with the 1992 election, a campaign's expenditures are allocable against a state limit only if they fall within one of five specific categories: media expenses, mass mailings, overhead expenses, special telephone programs, and public opinion polls. Any expenses outside of these categories do not have to be counted against a state's

TABLE 2.3

SPENDING LIMIT VIOLATIONS, 1976–1988

	Limit Exceeded[a]	Amount of Excess Spending ($)	Repayment ($)	% of Total Repayment[b]
1976 ELECTION				
Reagan	NH	30,285	30,285	4.9
Udall	NH	9,694	9,694	22.5
1980 ELECTION[c]				
Carter	IA	45,514	45,514	90.9
	NH	24,704	27,704	
	ME	28,075	28,075	
Kennedy	IA	40,611	13,562	100.0
	NH	14,889	4,972	
Reagan	NH	54,631	18,830	1.9
1984 ELECTION				
Cranston	IA	106,924	22,400	84.4
Glenn	IA	74,129	22,408	100.0
	NH	173,823	52,547	
Mondale[d]	IA	147,364	60,088	60.7
	NH	128,333	48,140	
	ME	25,283	—	
	US	578,904	68,000	
1988 ELECTION[e]				
Bush	IA	104,662	69,350	61.3
	NH	155,797		
	US	214,219		
Dole	IA	306,731	170,044	69.2
	NH	302,949		
Dukakis	IA	279,014	98,608	20.1
	NH	57,849		
DuPont	IA	77,447	25,775	100.0
Gephardt	IA	480,849	121,572	100.0
Kemp	IA	114,680	60,258	58.2
	NH	73,920		
Robertson	IA	635,683	338,632	87.2
	NH	506,108		
	US	659,970		
Simon	IA	885,585	366,389	88.6
	NH	219,832		

[a] This column notes the relevant state spending limit or, in the case of the designation "US," the overall national limit.

limit, although they do count against the national spending limit.[36] By contrast, the previous rules required allocation of all expenses unless an expense was covered by a specific exemption. The revised rules also automatically consider 10 percent of all administrative expenses within a state as exempt compliance spending.

The FEC has also simplified and significantly expanded the fundraising exemption. The new rules allow a campaign committee to treat up to 50 percent of the expenditures allocable to each state as fundraising expenses.[37] This means that a candidate can claim 50 percent of office overhead costs, media expenses, funds spent on special telephone programs designed to influence the voting in a particular state (such as voter registration or get-out-the-vote programs), and polling expenses, among others, as fundraising costs that are not allocable against a state's limit. In addition, a campaign can claim all of the costs associated with a mass mailing as exempt fundraising costs, so long as the expense is incurred 28 days before the date of a state's election. The overall cap on exempt fundraising expenditures, which is an amount equal to 20 percent of the national spending limit, is retained. Any sums spent on fundraising beyond this amount count against the national limit.

The new regulations have essentially turned the state limits into an accounting exercise. They allow such broad leeway in allocating costs that the limits should have little, if any, effect on a campaign's resource

---

[b] This column notes the percentage of a candidate's total repayment represented by the repayment assessed for excess spending.

[c] Originally, the Commission required repayment of an amount equal to the amount of excess spending. In accordance with a 1984 decision by the U.S. Court of Appeals for the District of Columbia, which was based on a case brought by the 1980 Kennedy and Reagan campaigns, the Commission established a policy that required repayment of only that portion of the excess expenditures that was paid with public funds.

[d] After a series of complex proceedings, the Mondale campaign was assessed a repayment of $60,088 for "exceeding state limits," a repayment of $29,640 and a penalty of $18,500 for delegate committee expenditures attributable to the New Hampshire limit, and a repayment of $68,000 for exceeding the overall limit.

[e] Beginning with the 1988 election, the FEC auditors have tended to assess one repayment sum for exceeding state limits based on the total amount of overspending. In cases where a candidate has violated both state and national limits, one repayment is assessed based on the larger of the two sums. In the two cases where this occurred in 1988, the larger sum was the amount in excess of state limits.

Source: Federal Election Commission, Final Audit Reports and Repayment Determinations.

decisions in the future. For example, in 1992 the New Hampshire limit was about $552,000. With the new 50 percent fundraising exemption and 10 percent compliance provision, the de facto ceiling is closer to $860,000, given the usual distribution of expenses in the New Hampshire race. Moreover, many of the most expensive items in a campaign are not counted against this amount. The costs associated with a candidate's travel and campaign appearances in the state, staff salaries, consultants' fees, and mass mailings conducted a month before the primary are considered exempt from the limit. In addition, candidates may still apportion only that share of the money spent on advertising that represents the potential New Hampshire audience against the state limit. Given these guidelines, a candidate can easily spend from $2.5 million to $3.5 million on the New Hampshire primary race, depending on the specific expenses incurred and the level of early spending, and still remain within the state's $552,000 cap.[38]

While candidates will now be able to spend large sums in Iowa and New Hampshire legally, this will probably have little effect on the dynamics of the presidential race or on the ability of lesser-known candidates to compete for the party's standard. Although the state limits were established in hopes of leveling the playing field in state elections, they have not had this effect. Candidates who have wanted to spend more in a state have found numerous ways to do so. As a result, the notion of a level playing field has never been realized in practice. Yet many lesser-known candidates, including Jimmy Carter and Ronald Reagan in 1976, Gary Hart in 1984, and Paul Tsongas in 1992, have still managed to wage viable campaigns. This suggests that it is more important to provide such candidates with the money needed to conduct a credible campaign than it is to limit the funds spent by potential frontrunners.

Furthermore, in future elections, the national spending limit will act as a restraint on state spending and reduce the possibility of a candidate winning the nomination by simply outspending an opponent by huge sums. The aggregate cap, not the state limits, will be the primary factor in a campaign's decision-making about how much to spend in a particular state. Candidates will have to balance their desire to win in Iowa and New Hampshire with their need to finance a competitive campaign for delegates in the other states. Some candidates will undoubtedly spend large sums early in the race in hopes of winning early and becoming the clear frontrunner. Regardless of the outcome, these candidates may place themselves in a vulnerable strategic position. If such a candidate fails to emerge as the frontrunner, he or she may lack the funds needed to maintain a viable campaign. If successful, he or she may face a challenger who can essentially spend more and run a more extensive campaign in the months ahead. Candidates will thus have to consider their spending patterns carefully and will not be able to focus all of their resources on one or two states.

The FEC reforms thus allow candidates more freedom to determine how to conduct their campaigns and eliminate much of the need to engage in subversive activities to avoid the political problems that might arise as a result of unrealistic state caps. They also relieve much of the accounting burden faced by candidates and commission auditors. The FEC, however, has gone about as far as it can to alleviate the counter-productive effects of the state ceilings. Congress should now follow these administrative reforms and further reduce the accounting burdens faced by candidates by eliminating these ceilings altogether.

CHAPTER THREE

FINANCING GENERAL
ELECTION CAMPAIGNS

T he financing of general election campaigns was supposed to be the simplest and most effective component of the public funding program. The terms of the scheme were fairly straightforward. Each of the major party candidates had to agree to abide by a national spending limit and had to refuse to accept private contributions.[1] In exchange, the government would provide a public grant equal to the full amount set by the spending limit. This amount was established under the 1974 law at $20 million per candidate adjusted for inflation; by 1992, the adjustments had raised the ceiling to $55.2 million per candidate. Public financing would thus replace private sources of revenue and free candidates from the need to spend time raising funds. It would eliminate the emphasis placed on money in general election campaigns and prevent the sorts of abuses that occurred before the FECA was adopted. Finally, it would reduce the costs of presidential campaigns since the combined amount that could be spent by the major party candidates, $40 million plus adjustments, was well below the $91.4 million total spent by Nixon and McGovern in the 1972 general election.[2]

Since 1976, every major presidential candidate has eagerly accepted public funding. The only candidate who could have qualified for public money yet refused to pursue this option was H. Ross Perot, the unlikely 1992 challenger who ran as an independent. Perot could have been eligible for a partial post-election of subsidy of more than $25 million, but he did not apply for it.[3] As one of America's few multibillionaires, he was wealthy enough to finance a competitive national campaign out of his own pocket. No other presidential nominee in modern electoral history has been so fortunate. Candidates have thus come to rely on public funding as the means by which they finance their campaigns.

By providing the resources needed to mount a national campaign, public financing has improved the electoral system in a number of ways. Candidates are no longer compelled to devote substantial amounts of time to incessant and burdensome fundraising responsibilities. Instead, they can focus their time and energy on campaigning and communicating their ideas to the voters. Public money has also helped to equalize the resources available to candidates, thereby creating a more level playing field in presidential elections. In addition, it has reduced the costs of a presidential campaign by eliminating fundraising expenses. Without the public subsidy, candidates would have to raise money on their own, which costs, on average, anywhere from 15 to 30 cents for each dollar raised. Public funding has thus saved tens of millions of dollars in fundraising expenses. This has allowed candidates to devote a greater share of their resources to television advertising and other methods of communicating their message to voters.

Despite these benefits, which should not be disregarded, public financing has failed to live up to its promise. It has not guaranteed full public disclosure of all monies spent in conjunction with a presidential election. It has not eliminated large "fat cat" contributions and the role of special interest money in national contests. It has not controlled spending. Nor has it put an end to public perceptions of the influence of wealthy donors and the inefficacy of an average citizen's role in the political system. As a result, public funding has not restored public faith in the integrity of the electoral process, which is the primary goal of any campaign finance law.

The reason why the system has fallen short of its objectives is not due to a flaw in the concept of public financing. The problem is that other provisions of the FECA have encouraged the development of a parallel system of private financing that has served to undermine the role of public money. Federal regulations allow national party committees to establish separate "nonfederal" accounts to finance activities conducted in association with state and local elections or party-building efforts.[4] These accounts differ from other party funds in that they are used to pay for activities that do not directly influence federal elections. The contributions deposited in these accounts are therefore subject only to state and local campaign finance laws, which are usually less restrictive than federal regulations. Party committees can use these accounts to accept contributions that would be considered illegal if given to a federal candidate. The FECA allows this practice in recognition of the national committees' traditional role as a source of assistance to state and local candidates and their traditional interest in developing party organizations at the state and local level.

Presidential candidates have exploited these provisions of the law to create a system of "soft money" financing designed to supplement public subsidies. This development has wholly undermined the basic purposes of the public funding program. Because a party's nonfederal funds are exempt from the regulations governing publicly funded candidates, they have prompted a return to the financial practices that characterized national elections before the FECA was adopted. The advent of soft money has allowed contributions of $100,000 or more from wealthy individuals, corporations, and labor unions to find their way back into the system. It has made a mockery of the spending limits imposed on presidential campaigns. It has encouraged the public to challenge the value of public funding and given millions of taxpayers cause to question the efficacy of contributing a dollar through the tax checkoff. The growth of soft money, therefore, has done more than diminish the efficacy of the public funding program: it has threatened the viability of the program itself.

THE RISE OF SOFT MONEY

"Soft money" is a general term used to describe any "money raised from sources outside the restraints of federal law but spent on activities intended to affect federal election outcomes."[5] While there are many kinds of soft money, in the context of presidential elections the term is usually used to describe the funds raised by the national party committees under the provisions of the 1979 FECA amendments. This form of soft money was established so that national party organizations could continue to fund grass-roots campaign activities and party-building efforts without violating the contribution and spending limits mandated by the campaign finance reforms. Although well-intentioned, the 1979 law has been used to create a system of political finance antithetical to the principles of campaign finance reform.

The 1979 reforms were designed to address some of the criticisms arising out of the experience of the 1976 election. Because spending was limited, Gerald Ford and Jimmy Carter each chose to concentrate their spending on media advertising rather than grass-roots political activities. Members of both parties complained that the law decreased the funds available for traditional volunteer activities such as canvassing, posting signs, and getting-out-the-vote on election day. Critics also argued that the law's contribution and spending limits had reduced the role of party organizations in presidential elections since these committees were no longer an important source of campaign revenue and were limited in what they could spend to assist the party's nominee.[6]

Congress responded to these concerns by adopting a recommendation made by the FEC to loosen the restrictions placed on contributions and spending so that party committees and other organizations could continue to finance grass-roots political activities. The new rules changed the law's definition of "contribution" and "expenditure" to exclude all monies used to conduct certain activities that were designed to promote grass-roots political participation in federal election campaigns. Such activities include the preparation and distribution of slate cards, sample ballots, and other listings of three or more candidates by state and local party committees; the production of campaign materials, such as pins, bumper stickers, brochures, and posters; and the carrying out of voter registration and turnout drives by state or local party organizations on behalf of their party's presidential ticket.[7]

The law thus created a new realm of unlimited funding by allowing party committees to spend two types of money in presidential elections. First, a party could spend the amount established under the law for "coordinated expenditures." This category of funds, which could be used for activities that directly benefit the party's nominee, has come to be known as "hard money" because it is governed by FECA limits and set at a sum equal to two cents times the voting age population. Second, a party could raise and spend soft money, which could essentially be used to supplement hard money expenditures. This category of funds, since it was exempt from federal limits, was governed by state campaign finance laws and was subject to no aggregate spending ceiling. Presidential campaigns could thus gain access to an unlimited source of funds by raising soft money at the national level and transferring sums to state and local parties for use on exempt activities.

It did not take long for presidential campaign staff members and party officials to recognize the possibilities inherent in the new regulations. Beginning with the 1980 election, members of a presidential nominee's fundraising staff were shifted to the national party's payroll at the end of the nomination process and given the task of working with party fundraisers to solicit soft money contributions. This allowed each party to solicit gifts from a broad donor base, since they could tap into the candidate's supporters as well as the party's traditional fundraising sources. The monies raised through these efforts could then be expended at the national level on activities carried out in conjunction with state and local organizations or directly channeled to state and local party committees for their use. Either way, the national party, which now included former members of the presidential candidate's campaign staff, could exercise control over the allocation of funds and devote them to purposes that would complement the strategic approaches being employed by the presidential campaign. This practice was allowable so long as the party's decisions were made independent of any influence from the candidate or campaign personnel.

The new rules also gave rise to another set of complicated allocation schemes. Since the amount of hard money that could be spent was limited, the parties began to allocate these funds in combination with soft money. The goal was to minimize hard money expenditures, while at the same time maximizing their effect. This principle of allocation between federal and nonfederal monies had already been established when the 1979 amendments were adopted by virtue of a number of FEC regulatory decisions made in cases involving state party committees.[8] These rulings declared that proportionate funding from federal and nonfederal sources was allowable so long as the allocations were made on some reasonable basis. For example, the Commission permitted a combination of hard and soft money that reflected the proportions spent on federal elections as compared to nonfederal elections. Parties could also allocate funds based on the number of candidates appearing on a state's ballot, provided that the federal candidates were given greater weight. Party organizations exploited these provisions and developed innovative funding schemes. These schemes often required that no more than a third of the amount spent on a coordinated activity be paid with hard money. The accounting practices employed by the national parties to take advantage of soft money thus began to mimic the practices used by presidential primary candidates to accommodate the state spending limits.

In an effort to end such practices and simplify the accounting process, the FEC in 1990 revised its regulations governing nonfederal funds. One of the major provisions of the new rules is a requirement that national party committees allocate a fixed 65 percent of their administrative expenses and voter drive costs as hard money expenses.[9] Fixed or minimum percentages are also established for other types of expenses. While these provisions have eliminated some of the more blatant abuses, they have had no significant effect on the flow of soft money in presidential elections.

Soft Money and the Campaign Finance System

The attractiveness of soft money is due to the state provisions concerning contribution limits. As of early 1992, 16 states placed no limit on the size of individual contributions. Nineteen states placed no limit on PAC contributions. Eleven states failed to limit corporate donations and one state, Massachusetts, placed no ceiling on labor union contributions. In addition, New York and Washington limit individual gifts, but their ceilings are set so high (up to $50,000 for statewide office) that they fail to discourage large donations.[10] State laws therefore facilitate soft money gifts in excess of the amounts permitted in federal elections and from sources (corporations and labor unions) that have long been banned from giving money to presidential campaigns.[11]

State campaign finance laws have also allowed most soft money activity to take place without effective public scrutiny. While all states have disclosure laws, the information required of candidates, contributors, and party committees differs greatly. In many states, the efficacy of the disclosure law is also undermined by poor administration. As of 1991, for example, only 13 states had established special commissions or agencies to enforce campaign finance and ethics laws, most of which are understaffed and underfinanced. In the remaining states, campaign reports are filed with various state officials and, in some instances, reports are not retained in one place. In Ohio, for example, disclosure reports for legislative candidates are retained in the state's 64 counties instead of in the state capital.[12] Even if these reports were collected in one place, the information is often neither readily accessible nor compiled in a comprehensible form. Consequently, much of the soft money activity that occurs at the state level remains in the shadows, concealed from even the most dogged investigators.

This lack of effective disclosure at the state level has been compounded by the inadequacy of federal regulations. Up until 1990, the FEC did not require national party committees to disclose the transactions conducted through their nonfederal accounts. The FEC took an initial step toward correcting this problem in its revised 1990 regulations, which imposed stricter reporting requirements on nonfederal accounts. These guidelines require national committees to disclose soft money contributors of $200 or more, and to report the transactions conducted through nonfederal accounts. Committees therefore have to disclose the uses of soft money and the amounts transferred to state and local party committees. But the rules do not extend to the soft money directly contributed to nonfederal candidates. These transactions remain under the jurisdiction of state legislation.

Given the inadequacy of disclosure laws, it is impossible to determine precisely how much soft money has been spent in conjunction with presidential elections or where the funds have come from. The Citizens' Research Foundation, however, has estimated the amounts spent in each election during the 1980s, based on the available public records, private reports, and information voluntarily released by the national party committees. More detailed information is available for the 1992 election as a result of the FEC's new disclosure regulations.

In 1980 and 1984, the Republicans took greater advantage of soft money than the Democrats. According to the Citizens' Research Foundation, the Republicans raised an average $15 million in soft

money in each of these elections, or about three times more than the
Democrats (see Table 3.1). Of the $15 million raised by the Republicans
in 1980, about $9 million was raised at the national level and funneled
to state and local committees. The other $6 million was raised by state
and local committees for use on activities that would benefit the
Republican ticket. The Democrats also established a soft money operation in 1980 but were much less successful. They managed to raise only
about $4 million, with $1.3 million solicited nationally from labor
unions and wealthy individuals and the rest coming from the fundraising efforts of state and local parties.[13]

In 1984, soft money became a focal point of public attention as news-
paper accounts began to report the plans being developed by both parties to make soft money an important component of their general election strategies. These reports drew great attention because of the huge
sums that were purportedly involved, with pre-election estimates ranging anywhere from $25 million for the Democrats to more than $50 million for the Republicans.[14] The actual amounts received by the parties
were much lower. As in 1980, the Republicans generated about $15 mil-
lion in soft money. This included $5.6 million raised nationally by the
Republican National Committee, which was transferred to state and local
committees; $5 million raised by state and local committees on their own
from their own sources; and $5 million raised by the Republican National
State Elections Committee, a separate committee created by the Republican

TABLE 3.1

ESTIMATED SOFT MONEY EXPENDITURES, 1980–1992
($ MILLIONS)

Election	Republican	Democrat
1980	15.1	4.0
1984	15.6	6.0
1988	22.0	23.0
1992	33.1	30.0

Note: The amounts for 1980–1988 are based on estimates by the Citizens'
Research Foundation. The 1992 figures are based on FEC disclosure reports for
the Democratic and Republican National Committee Non-Federal Accounts and
exclude monies raised for building funds and the Democratic Non-Federal News
Service.

Source: Citizens' Research Foundation and Federal Election Commission.

National Committee to support state and local candidates using funds that were not subject to the provisions of the FECA.[15]

The Democrats took a more aggressive approach to soft money fundraising in 1984 in hopes of reducing the advantage the Republicans had enjoyed in the previous race. A month after Walter Mondale's nomination, the party established the Democratic Victory Fund, a separate financial operation of the Democratic National Committee, which was responsible for raising hard and soft money for the general election. The Fund established four separate accounts designed to accommodate different types of soft money contributions: one account was set up for contributions from individuals who had already given the maximum amount under federal law, another for corporate contributions, a third for labor donations, and finally a "general" account. How much money was ultimately raised by the Democrats is difficult to assess. The Citizens' Research Foundation estimates that the Victory Fund raised $6 million in soft money.[16] This figure probably underestimates the Democrats' soft money resources since it does not include funds raised by state and local party committees. After the election, a party official noted that the four soft money accounts had received $9.4 million in corporate, union, and other contributions, but this total included some money that had been raised in 1983.[17] Whatever the final number, the Democrats did raise more soft money in 1984 than they had in 1980, but they still failed to match the amount raised by their Republican opponents.

Scattered reports published after the 1980 and 1984 elections noted that both parties had received large soft money contributions from individuals, corporations, and labor unions that greatly exceeded the amounts permitted in federal elections under the provisions of the FECA. In 1984, for example, the Democrats had received at least three individual gifts of $100,000 apiece and two labor unions had each contributed over $300,000 in nonfederal funds. The Republicans also received a significant number of large gifts, including a number of individual donations of $25,000 or more and dozens of $10,000 to $20,000 corporate donations.[18] Yet the role of these gifts and their importance as a source of revenue in presidential elections was not truly understood until the 1988 election, when large donations became a staple of soft money fundraising in both parties.

When Robert Farmer, Michael Dukakis's chief fundraiser during the presidential nomination campaign, took charge of the Democratic party's fundraising efforts in anticipation of the 1988 election, he was determined to make sure that his party was not outspent by the Republicans in the presidential contest. Farmer therefore established a fundraising goal of $50 million for the national committee, much of which would be solicited in the form of soft money. In order to reach this goal in the short time available between the Democratic convention and election day, Farmer emphasized the solicitation of $100,000 donations or the recruitment of individuals who would agree to raise $100,000. Robert Mosbacher, Bush's chief fundraiser and Farmer's Republican party counterpart, responded to the Democrats' challenge by establishing a major soft money drive within his own party. The primary component of this program was an effort to recruit members for a group called Team 100, which would consist of individuals or other donors who were willing to give at least $100,000 to party coffers.[19] With the terms of the contest set, the race was on.

Both parties openly and avidly pursued large checks from "fat cats" in 1988 and thus raised more soft money than in the two previous races combined. Overall, the Democrats met Farmer's objective, raising $23 million in soft money as compared to $22 million for the Republicans. With respect to big givers, the Republicans claimed 267 contributors of $100,000 or more, and the Democrats counted 130 individuals who gave or raised $100,000 or more.[20] The Democrats probably would have had more large donors were it not for the influence of their nominee. Dukakis instructed Farmer that no soft money donations in excess of $100,000 should be accepted and that no gifts were to be accepted from corporations, labor unions, and PACs. This stipulation placed some of the Democrats' most reliable soft money sources off limits and forced Farmer to rely on the largesse of wealthy individuals for all nationally raised nonfederal funds. The party did, however, accept a number of soft money contributions before Dukakis was nominated that violated these restrictions, including a $1 million gift from Joan Kroc, the widow of the founder of the McDonald's Corporation.[21]

The Republicans pursued soft money donations without any self-imposed restrictions and thus were able to solicit a greater number of large gifts, which is not surprising, given the party's traditional support among wealthy donors. But they also enjoyed the advantage of being able to solicit corporations and PACs, two sources the Democrats had decided to avoid. The Republicans particularly benefited from their success in soliciting gifts from corporations, which represented about a third of their Team 100 donors.[22] Some of the Team 100 members gave more than their required minimum, including former ambassador to Hungary Nicholas Salgo, who gave $503,263, which was described at the time as the Republican's "largest known political gift since the 1972 Nixon campaign."[23]

In 1992, both parties generally followed the approaches established in 1988. Once again, a premium was placed on large contributions as a means of generating soft money. There were, however, two important differences. First, the Republicans sought to build on the success of their Team

100 approach by maintaining the program and asking Team 100 members to donate $25,000 a year during each of the four years in the presidential election cycle and an additional $100,000 in the election year.[24] This approach, in theory, would allow them to raise more soft money early in the presidential cycle without significantly reducing the amounts raised in the election year. The net effect would therefore be a substantial increase in the amount of soft money received in a four-year period and more money available for use in conjunction with the congressional mid-term elections.

Second, the Democrats were not constrained by self-imposed limitations on their soft money operation. Bill Clinton did not follow Dukakis's example and limit the size or sources of soft money gifts. The Democratic National Committee was therefore able to tap into the full range of potential soft money donors, including corporations, labor unions, and PACs. This task was made easier by the political prospects of their nominee. Unlike previous elections, Bill Clinton held a substantial lead in public opinion polls throughout most of the general election campaign. The excitement surrounding the probability of a Democratic victory for the first time in over a decade encouraged many contributors, including some Team 100 members, to give large sums in support of the Democratic ticket.

Overall, the 1992 election was the fourth consecutive contest to witness significant growth in the amount of soft money raised by the national party committees. According to the reports filed with the FEC, the Republicans raised a total of $33.1 million in soft money and the Democrats raised $30 million (see Table 3.1).[25] While both parties began to raise soft money well in advance of the election, the major portion of these funds was received in the four-month period leading up to election day. The Republicans fared better early in the election cycle, raising about $20 million compared to the Democrats' $9 million between January 1, 1991, and July 1, 1992. Thereafter, the Democrats surpassed the Republicans by a substantial margin, raising about $20.1 million to the Republicans' estimated $12.8 million from July 1 through to election day. Another $730,000 in soft money was received by the Democrats just after the election.[26]

As in 1988, big givers were the key to success in raising soft money funds. A Common Cause study of the soft money contributions received by the Democratic National Committee revealed that 72 contributors had donated $100,000 or more, including 23 who gave more than $150,000. The Democrats received gifts of more than $200,000 from seven individuals and five labor unions, including $398,876 from the United Steelworkers and $344,180 from the National Education Association. They also received 17 corporate contributions of $100,000 or more, including $171,573 from the Atlantic Richfield Company and $152,000 from the Philip Morris Company.[27] The Common Cause study did not examine soft money gifts to the Republican National Committee, but FEC reports show that more than 60 contributors gave at least $100,000 in soft money.[28] These included a combined total of $977,000 from the Archer-Daniels-Midland Corporation and its chair, Dwayne Andreas; $520,300 from the Atlantic Richfield Company; and $450,000 from Edgar Bronfman, whose company, Seagrams and Sons, gave an additional $58,727.

While the number of large contributors reported in 1992 was significantly lower than the number reported in 1988, this does not mean that the parties placed less reliance on wealthy individuals in seeking soft money gifts. The Democrats actively sought $100,000 donors, but they also allowed individuals to meet this commitment by raising $100,000 for the party. One report, which included both groups, estimated that the Democrats had about two hundred and fifty $100,000 "donors."[29] Also, the FEC disclosure reports only include contributions made in 1991 and 1992. Republican Team 100 members who donated $100,000 via annual payments of $25,000 would therefore not be reported as $100,000 givers.

Soft money contributions have made a shambles of the contribution and spending limits imposed on presidential general election campaigns. More importantly, they present a serious challenge to the notion that wealthy individuals and interest groups no longer enjoy special influence as a result of their contributions. For example, in a study of the 1988 Team 100 members, Common Cause noted numerous instances of soft money donors who represented businesses with important regulatory concerns or substantial matters pending before federal agencies.[30] Upon reviewing this information, the authors of the report concluded:

> Almost across the board, Team 100 members or the companies they are associated with want something from the government—whether it's broad policy initiatives like Bush's proposed reduction in the capital gains tax or favors more specific to a company or industry. Many gave their $100,000 at a time when they had significant business or regulatory matters pending with the federal government—or knew they likely would under the Bush administration. . . . [T]here's a perception problem—and a risk of more than that. When an individual who has served as a presidential candidate's chief fundraiser seeks huge contributions from corporations, or their executives, it raises fundamental questions in the public's mind. Did the contributors give in an effort to influence government decisions? And will such contributions ultimately have this effect?[31]

Common Cause sought to answer these questions in a subsequent investigation. This study revealed dozens of regulatory decisions by the Bush administration that benefited soft money contributors and identified a number of soft money givers who had been nominated to serve as ambassadors or as members of regulatory commissions.[32] In no instance, however, did Common Cause find any wrongdoing or improper action on the part of a federal agency, a member of the administration, or a soft money donor.

Soft money contributors typically deny that their donations are linked to some quid pro quo or desire for special influence. Since the practice was formalized in 1980, no presidential soft money donor has been judged guilty of any improper action or been shown to have received special consideration because of a donation. The problem with large soft money gifts has not been that they have led to massive corruption in the political system. Rather, it is that they encourage the appearance of corruption and widespread public perceptions that wealthy interests enjoy undue influence in the political process. With corporations and labor unions giving hundreds of thousands of dollars to be used in presidential elections, the public can reach no other conclusion than that such gifts come with strings attached.

The perception that soft money is given for purposes of influence is fed by the actions of some donors, who appear to be "covering their bases." In 1988, for example, at least eight donors gave $100,000 to each of the major parties.[33] Similarly, in 1992, a number of contributors gave major sums to each party. In some cases, these contributions were made late in the race as the likelihood of a Democratic victory increased. For example, Archer-Daniels-Midland donated $90,000 to the Democratic National Committee through seven subsidiaries four days before the election, after giving close to $1 million to the Republican National Committee. Edgar Bronfman, one of the leading Team 100 members, gave $200,000 to the Democrats in early October, as did the Revlon Corporation, which balanced $140,000 in contributions to Republicans with $120,000 in checks to the Democrats.[34] And these cases were not unique. A study conducted by the nonpartisan Center for Responsive Politics found that donors representing five traditionally Republican industries shifted their patterns of giving in the period after the Democratic National Convention. In three industries (investment and securities; pharmaceuticals and health; and beer, wine, and liquor), soft money contributions shifted from an average of three- or four-to-one in favor of the Republicans to an advantage in favor of the Democrats, while in two others (oil and gas, and insurance), the gap between Republicans and Democrats narrowed significantly. Ellen Miller, director of the Center, said the study "confirms the investment theory of politics. . . . These industries want to invest in the next president for access and influence. When they saw the tide turn to Clinton, they began to use their money as an investment."[35]

Supporters of soft money financing argue that the new disclosure laws will rid the system of any potential corruption because all contributions will now be subject to full public scrutiny. Disclosure is undoubtedly an essential tool for guarding against abuse and ensuring effective enforcement of the law. It also helps to ensure that voters have the knowledge they need to make an informed choice when casting their ballots.

Yet, because of the size of the contributions involved, disclosure has also served to promote public perceptions of the influence of wealthy interests. As more information has been revealed about soft money and the role of large contributors, the public has had more reason to question the integrity of the system. Soft money has thus encouraged the view that presidential elections continue to be dominated by special interests and that individual participation plays little role in determining electoral outcomes. While soft money is not the only source of these attitudes, this widely publicized form of finance has certainly had a major impact on the public's thinking. Instead of restoring public confidence, the campaign finance laws have provoked the very attitudes they were supposed to put to rest and have thereby undermined support for the public funding system.

THE ROLE OF SOFT MONEY

Public debate on the role of soft money in the political system has focused almost exclusively on the sources of these funds. Overshadowed in these discussions is the original purpose of the law, which was to provide party organizations with a meaningful form of participation in national elections. This lack of attention to the uses of soft money is in large part a consequence of inadequate disclosure laws, which make any sort of authoritative information on how parties disburse these funds difficult to obtain. While some studies have provided specific examples of soft money spending, these efforts often fail to achieve even a broad outline of the contours of soft money finance.[36] A better understanding of soft money activities is now possible due to the disclosure reports filed by the FEC. Even these reports, however, fail to provide a complete picture of the role of soft money in national elections.

For decades, knowledgeable political observers have expressed concern over the declining role of party organizations in America. The 1979 FECA amendments represent a step toward addressing this problem by providing the national committees with a means of funding joint activity with state and local organizations. This law was not, as many critics claim, a purposeful decision to create a "loophole" in federal regulations. It was a conscious effort on the part of the Congress to empower state and local party committees in federal campaigns. While the activities financed with soft money, which include voter registration and mobilization programs, have primarily been designed to assist the presidential ticket, they also help to promote the development of state and local party organizations and stimulate citizen participation in the electoral process.

In 1992, the national party committees spent soft money funds on four broad types of political activity: direct transfer payments to state and local parties, contributions to state and local candidates, joint federal and nonfederal activities, and miscellaneous expenditures reported as "other spending" (see Table 3.2). In general, the Republicans concentrated spending on joint activities and direct contributions to candidates. The Democrats also spent a substantial portion of their funds on joint activities, but allocated more of their money in the form of direct cash transfers to state and local party committees. This was in part due to transfers made by the Democratic National Committee to provide state parties with their share of the funds raised through "Democratic Party Victory Fund" events. It may also be the case that the Democratic state party committees are not as well-financed as their Republican counterparts and thus have a greater need for assistance from the national party. The Republicans also devoted a larger sum to "other spending," in part because the party reported hundreds of thousands of dollars of in-kind media and consulting expenditures made on behalf of its 1991 gubernatorial candidates in this category. The Republican National Committee's miscellaneous spending also included $2.57 million in building fund expenditures for its party headquarters, as compared to less than $100,000 in building expenses for the Democrats.[37]

Both national committees adopted strongly centralized approaches in administering these funds in an effort to maintain control over the

TABLE 3.2

NATIONAL SOFT MONEY ACCOUNT DISBURSEMENTS, 1992 ($)

Party	Transfers to State Parties	Contributions to State/Local Candidates	Share of Joint Activity	Other Spending
Democrat	9,495,328	212,091	17,997,293	2,483,201
Republican	5,338,595	1,249,000	19,792,098	9,248,215

Source: Federal Election Commission.

ways soft money was spent. Even in the case of monies transferred to state and local party organizations, the national committees allowed little autonomy with respect to how the funds were to be spent. In most instances, transferred funds were to be used on projects approved by the national organization.

The major share of soft money funds in both parties was devoted to joint activity, that is, to activities that were designed to influence both federal and nonfederal elections. Examples include the costs of fundraising efforts designed to raise soft and hard money; the administrative expenses associated with soft money operations; the monies paid for generic campaign materials and advertisements that say "Vote Democratic" or "Vote Republican"; and expenses for phone banks and other voter identification and turnout projects that assist party candidates at all levels.

The most prominent form of joint activity is generic advertising, especially television advertising. In 1992, both parties invested heavily in this tactic, paying for the production and broadcast of ads with a combination of hard and soft money funds. Overall, the Democrats spent about $14.2 million on ads and the Republicans spent about $10 million.[38] The Republicans basically followed the strategy employed in previous elections, since they have always spent substantial amounts of soft money on generic advertising. For the Democrats, however, this emphasis on party advertising represented a new approach to general election campaigning. While the party did broadcast some ads in 1988, the total amount spent was only $1 million.[39]

Generic advertising allows the national committees to build support for their respective parties and communicate major issues to the voters, which benefits party candidates running for office at all levels of government. It can be especially beneficial to the presidential ticket, particularly when the ads are designed to reinforce the party nominee's message. The Democrats, for example, used soft money to finance ads that did not mention Bill Clinton directly (since this would violate federal regulations) but did hammer home the message on the economy that was the foundation of Clinton's campaign.[40] These ads also helped to free up resources that the Clinton campaign could use for other purposes. During the last week of the campaign, for instance, the Clinton campaign was running short of money and thus decided to use campaign resources to buy a half-hour of national television time as opposed to additional broadcast time in the highly competitive state of Texas. The campaign, however, did not leave Texas unattended; instead, the national committee broadcast generic ads in the state to spread the party's message. The Bush campaign adopted a similar strategy, relying on party ads to shore up support in traditional Republican strongholds and in crucial battleground states like Texas and Florida.[41]

Soft money was also used by both parties to defray the administrative or overhead expenses of the national party operation. For example, because most national party staff members spend at least some time working with state party officials or assisting individuals involved in nonfederal political activities, both parties use soft money to pay for 35 to 40 percent of their national payroll. This purpose, which is considered a joint activity disbursement, represents a sizeable soft money expense. In 1991, the Democrats spent about $1.6 million in soft money on payroll expenses, while the Republicans spent about $2.4 million. Soft money has thus helped facilitate the expansion and professionalization of national party staffs. As a result, the national parties can offer more services to their constituents. Perhaps more importantly, this practice also helps to free up hard dollars, which can then be used for such purposes as coordinated spending to assist candidates, rather than to pay the bills at the national headquarters.

Parties also raise soft money as a vehicle for providing direct financial assistance to state and local committees. In 1992, about a quarter of the funds raised nationally by the two major parties were transferred to state and local party committees. These funds provide state and local party organizations with the resources needed to conduct activities that they would otherwise not be able to afford. These funds are often used to purchase, update, and computerize voter lists; to develop targeting programs; to pay fundraising expenses; and to hire party workers and poll watchers on election day. While both parties spent money on these types of activities in 1992, the bulk of the funds transferred to state parties were used for generic phone bank programs designed to identify party supporters and turn out the vote.

According to FEC disclosure reports, most of the state party organizations received a share of the soft money funds raised by their respective national party committees. The Democrats transferred almost $9.5 million in nonfederal funds to 47 states.[42] Federal funds were sent to all 50 states. With this hard money added, the total amount sent to state committees was $14.3 million. The Republicans sent about $5.3 million in nonfederal monies to 42 states and about $3.5 million in federal funding to 43 states, for a total of about $8.8 million.[43]

Most of the soft money sent to state committees was focused on a small group of targeted states that were considered essential to a presidential victory. As noted in Table 3.3, the Democrats disbursed two-thirds of the nonfederal funds sent to states in ten key electoral battlegrounds. These ten states, which contained 219 electoral college votes or 81 percent of the total needed to win, included most of the large electoral states and three crucial Southern states that the Democrats thought they could win—Georgia, Louisiana, and North Carolina. The Republicans also disbursed two-thirds of their transfer funds in ten states. These states, which contained 190 electoral votes or 70 percent of the number needed to win, also included a number of large states and three key Southern contests. The one "oddity" on the list of top Republican states was North Dakota. But North Dakota was an important state for the Republicans in 1992 since it was viewed as a needed "base" state in the presidential election and was the site of a key gubernatorial contest that the party ultimately won.

Federal disclosure reports reveal some major differences between the two parties in their use of soft money to assist party organizations and candidates. One of the problems the Republican party has faced in recent decades is its lack of success in gubernatorial and state legislative elections. Despite winning five of six presidential races, the Republicans have failed to capture a majority of the nation's state houses. As part of the effort to reverse this pattern, the Republicans transferred funds to state legislative campaign committees, as well as the state party committee, in at least fifteen states. This approach, if it succeeds in helping to elect Republicans to state legislative office, will not only improve Republican voting strength in state assemblies, but in the

TABLE 3.3

SOFT MONEY TRANSFERS TO STATE AND LOCAL PARTIES, 1992[a]

	Top Ten Democratic States			Top Ten Republican States	
1	California	1,204,814	1	Ohio	968,891
2	Texas	1,035,383	2	California	492,150
3	Pennsylvania	637,935	3	North Carolina	325,452
4	Georgia	632,711	4	Georgia	292,860
5	New York	611,885	5	Michigan	289,825
6	North Carolina	582,633	6	Washington	256,725
7	Ilinois	459,539	7	North Dakota	253,775
8	Louisiana	373,914	8	South Carolina	239,500
9	Michigan	339,694	9	Pennsylvania	227,381
10	Missouri	332,387	10	Florida	222,432
Total		6,210,895			3,568,991
% of All Soft Money Transfers		65.4			66.8

[a] Figures represent the dollar amounts of non-federal funds transferred from the Democratic and Republican National Committees.

Source: Federal Election Commission.

long term may help the party to improve its pool of candidates for statewide office and congressional contests.

In addition, the Republicans directly contributed a total of $1.2 million in nonfederal funds to candidates seeking office at the state level. During the 1992 general election period, the party contributed about $804,000 to candidates in 23 states. Most of these funds were used to assist the Republican nominee in key gubernatorial contests. About $550,000, or about 68 percent of the soft monies donated to candidates, was given to gubernatorial candidates in five states (Missouri, New Hampshire, North Dakota, Utah, and Washington). The leading recipient was William Webster, the party's nominee in Missouri, who was given $225,000, while Ken Eikenberry of Washington received $125,000 and Edward Schafer of North Dakota received $95,000. Other major gifts included $20,000 for the Pennsylvania Attorney General's race and $21,000 for legislative candidates in Georgia.

The Democrats spent none of their soft money during the 1992 general election period on direct contributions to candidates. Although the committee reported about $148,000 in contributions to candidates during the general election period, this sum actually represented the funds expended to provide survey research to state parties and candidates. The Democratic National Committee hired six Washington-based polling firms, including the firm of Stanley Greenberg, the Clinton campaign pollster, to conduct surveys in 31 states. In 27 of these states, polls were conducted at least two or three times during the course of the campaign.[44] The results were shared with state party officials so that they could target their appeals and voter canvassing efforts. The polls also included questions related to particular state races and these results were provided to these campaigns. In addition to gubernatorial candidates, the party-sponsored polling gathered information for some of the candidates seeking the office of lieutenant governor, attorney general, secretary of state, state auditor, associate justice, and, in Texas, railroad commissioner. This research was financed through a combination of hard and soft money, with part of the expense included in the amounts reported as transfer payments and another part counted as contributions to candidates.

Soft money thus allowed the Democrats to provide state parties with a resource, statewide polling data, that most of these organizations could not otherwise afford. This service offered a number of benefits. First, it provided high-quality survey research to many party organizations and candidates. Such information aids in the development of more effective communications with voters and helps parties and candidates target their resources more efficiently. Second, it freed up funds for other purposes and reduced the aggregate amounts spent on survey research. By conducting a coordinated, centralized polling operation, the Democrats eliminated the need for duplicative efforts by different candidates. While some candidates still conducted their own polling, they could reduce the amount their campaigns had to spend on survey research by "piggybacking" onto a poll that was primarily being conducted to allow the Democrats to track the progress of the presidential race. Or to take another perspective, it allowed the Clinton campaign to gain access to the information it needed on the status of the race in targeted states without having to bear the full cost of these polls. This sharing of information thus reduced the aggregate amount the presidential campaign had to spend on polling, or at least gave it more bang for its buck.

It should be noted, however, that polling services were not the only means by which the Democrats used soft money to assist their candidates. In 1991, for example, the party used soft money in a number of ways to assist its candidates in Pennsylvania. According to FEC reports, the Democratic National Committee transferred $50,000 from its non-federal individual account to the Pennsylvania Democratic Party between August and October. It also directly contributed $25,000 to Ed Rendell, the party's candidate in the Philadelphia mayoral race. In the special election for United States Senator, the party supplemented its coordinated spending made on behalf of its candidate, Harris Wofford, by spending $50,000 in soft money funds on media expenses and by paying a portion of the salaries, per diem expenses, and travel costs of a dozen party organizers who were sent to Pennsylvania to help coordinate an election day get-out-the-vote program.

This brief outline of the role of soft money in 1992 exemplifies some of the major issues in the soft money debate. Advocates claim that soft money gives the party organizations a meaningful role in federal elections. It allows the national parties to place themselves in the role of financial broker and provide sorely needed resources and services to committees and candidates at all levels of government. In many instances, state and local parties would not be able to carry out grass-roots activities without these funds. By providing the monies needed to develop voter files and outreach programs that help more than one candidate, soft money encourages candidates to work with local party members and helps to stimulate grass-roots political activity. Since these activities do not simply benefit the presidential candidate, it is appropriate that their financing is not based solely on federally limited funds. Moreover, when the dust from the presidential election has settled, the state organization is left with materials and experience that can be used to assist candidates in other elections or serve as the foundation for future party-building efforts.

Critics note that these activities are primarily conducted for the benefit of the presidential candidate, with the funds raised by the candidate's former staff and the expenditures determined by individuals aware of the campaign's strategy. This, they allege, violates the intent of the campaign finance laws and public funding, since soft money spending amounts to little more than a thinly veiled means of channeling private funds into presidential campaigns.[45] Consequently, soft money has diminished the value of campaign spending limits since it allows campaign organizations to spend significantly more than the amount established by public subsidies.

Presidential campaigns have certainly exercised more influence over soft money allocations than might have been anticipated. Soft money has also allowed presidential campaigns to shift some of their traditional expenses to the national committee budget. For example, state party voter canvassing and mobilization programs perform much of the work usually carried out by a presidential candidate's field operation. With the rise of soft money, presidential campaigns have scaled back their general election field programs, essentially shifting these costs to party committees and thereby freeing up funds for television advertising and travel. Soft money has also been used to defray polling expenses and served as a supplement to campaign advertising budgets.

The FEC has acknowledged the role of soft money in presidential campaigns and taken a first step toward addressing critics' concerns with its new allocation regulations. These rules require that parties pay for the major share of some joint activities with federal funds in recognition of the relative advantage federal candidates can gain from such expenditures. Furthermore, while soft money has assisted presidential candidates, it has not been used for wholly unintended purposes. Although the original provisions of the public funding program essentially sought to eliminate the role of private funding in general elections, Congress changed the law in 1979 to permit spending that indirectly benefited presidential contenders because they felt such spending was needed in order to ensure a continued role for party organizations. Soft money has fulfilled this purpose by providing the means by which parties can participate in national elections and assist their candidates at all levels of government.

The rise of soft money has thus led to the renewal of a realm of political activity in which national and state parties work together in the pursuit of common electoral goals. As Frank Sorauf and Scott Wilson have observed, with their new role as financial brokers, "the parties have begun to win back some of their lost role in electoral politics."

> Their ability to raise money and to direct the raising of money from others has made the parties the active players in campaign politics that they were not in the 1960s and 1970s. (That rebound has also resulted, of course, from the development of the parties' capacity to provide

campaign technologies and services.) Thus they have "adapted," even recouped a bit, in a campaign politics dominated by candidates and new technologies and technocrats.[46]

Sorauf and Wilson further note, however, that this new financial power
has not produced the type of responsible, policy-based political parties
that many observers desire and hold out as the key to diminishing the
influence of special interests and providing the electorate with meaningful choices in political campaigns. Party committees have not yet moved
beyond their modest electoral aim of victories in key contests to the broader goal of tying spending in campaigns "to the candidate's position on
issues, program or ideology or to the candidate's record of support for
party positions."[47] Even so, soft money has served an important role in
the reemergence of national party organizations. This type of financing
should thus be continued in the future, albeit it in a modified form that
eliminates the problems experienced in the past.

CHAPTER FOUR

THE FUTURE OF REFORM

Public financing is one of the boldest political reforms ever adopted by Congress. Like most reforms, its implementation has led to intended and unintended consequences. As a result, further reform of the campaign finance system is needed if public financing is to fulfill its original promise.

The experience with public funding in the past five elections has revealed three major problems with the system. First, even with the recent increase in the amount of the income tax checkoff, the public subsidies program faces the prospect of a future financial shortfall due to a structural imbalance between payments and contributions, and declining participation. Without reform, the program will eventually become insolvent. Second, the expenditure ceilings that accompany public subsidies have failed to control spending. While some candidates have restricted their spending to conform to the law, the primary effect of these limits has been to encourage candidates to engage in creative accounting and develop ingenious methods of circumventing the law. Finally, the system has not eliminated the influence of large donors in general election campaigns. This failure poses the greatest threat to the legitimacy of the system since it has fueled public cynicism and encouraged taxpayers to lose faith in the tax checkoff as a means of improving campaign finance.

The past five elections have also demonstrated the value of public financing. Perhaps the best way to envision the benefits of public money is to consider what the system would be like without it. In other words, what would happen if Congress adopted one of the many bills introduced in recent years by those who oppose public financing and abolished the Presidential Election Campaign Fund and the public funding program?

Under this circumstance, presidential candidates would be governed by regulations similar to those now placed on congressional candidates. Presidential aspirants would still be subject to the FECA's disclosure requirements and contribution limits, but in all likelihood, they would not be subject to spending limits since the Supreme Court has ruled that these restrictions are only justified if a candidate is receiving public funds. Presidential contenders would be allowed to raise and spend as much as they could, so long as their contributions were in compliance with federal law and duly reported. The financing of presidential elections would, therefore, probably come to be characterized by many of the problems found in congressional elections, writ large.

Without public funding, presidential candidates would have to devote most of their time to the burdensome task of raising money. This would be especially true in general election campaigns. Because the federal limits on contributions would still apply, candidates would have to raise the tens of millions of dollars needed to finance a viable campaign through individual donations of no more than $1,000 and PAC contributions of no more than $5,000. To raise even the minimum amount needed for a nationwide campaign would require the solicitation of tens of thousands of donations and a base of donors far more extensive than the base needed for a primary campaign. Even worse, a substantial portion of the monies raised would have to be spent on fundraising, thus increasing the total costs of a campaign and the amount that has to be amassed in order to have the funds needed to pay for television advertising and other expensive, but necessary, campaign technologies.

General election fundraising would be especially onerous due to the limited time period that would be available to most candidates. Observers of congressional elections, including many members of the House and Senate, have vociferously complained of the fundraising pressures generated by the campaign finance system. Critics have traced a wide range of problems to a system in which a senator "must" raise an average of $10,000 to $15,000 a week and a member of Congress "must" begin seeking funds for reelection shortly after election day. These pressures would be greatly exacerbated in a presidential contest. A candidate could not practically begin to raise general election money until his or her nomination was secured. At best, most candidates would have less than six months to fill their campaign coffers, which translates into a need to raise *at least* one to two million dollars a week, or one hundred times the average amount needed for a senate race. This might have been possible in the days prior to the FECA, when wealthy donors could give a million dollars or more, as W. Clement Stone did in donating $2 million to Nixon's reelection campaign. But those days are now gone, as are unlimited contributions from national party committees, which were another key source of revenue for presidential nominees in the pre-FECA era.

While some observers might note that candidates already spend time raising soft money during the general election, this commitment in no way compares to the amount of time that would be consumed in a wholly privately funded system. Indeed, at most, the candidates now spend a relatively small portion of their time attending fundraising events for their respective parties. In most cases, the candidates attend fewer than two dozen events and, in 1988, Democratic vice-presidential candidate Lloyd Bentsen attended no soft money fundraisers at all.[1] In a privately funded system, candidates would have to attend fundraisers and spend time soliciting money on an almost daily basis, and it would not be unusual for a candidate to spend up to a third or more of his or her time seeking contributions. As a result, much less time would be available for personal campaigning and communicating with voters.

To meet the resource demands of a national campaign, candidates would have to place greater emphasis on PAC donations and soft money. Presidential candidates would probably turn to PACs as a key source of funding as soon as their nominations were assured, since it is more efficient to raise money in $5,000 sums than in $1,000 gifts. Soft money would become even more important, because it would be the only source of revenue in the system that could provide the huge sums needed for a national campaign. National party committees probably would feel compelled to assume an increasingly large share of the costs of a presidential campaign and finance as many activities as possible with soft money. This would not only relieve some of the fundraising burden faced by the nominee, but it would also help to ensure that the party's choice is able to wage a competitive campaign.

Private financing would therefore dramatically enhance the potential influence of wealthy donors and interests, since their soft money gifts would play an increasingly important role in the overall financing of a presidential campaign. In addition, these wealthy donors would be able to raise money directly for a presidential candidate by serving as principal fundraisers for the nominee's campaign committee. This dual role would allow them to improve their links to the candidate and would almost certainly solidify public perceptions of the influence of wealthy interests in the electoral process.

Congress could diminish this potential consequence of a solely private system by adopting further restrictions on PAC giving and the use of soft money. These reforms might reduce the influence of wealthy donors but, at the same time, they would intensify the fundraising burden placed on candidates. To compensate for the potential revenue lost from PACs and soft money contributions, candidates would have to place even greater reliance on individual gifts, which would increase the amount of time they would need to devote to fundraising. They would thus have even less time to spend on personal campaigning and communicating with voters. Or they could simply reduce their campaign spending to accommodate limited resources. Most candidates, however, would probably accomplish this by reducing their staff, campaign travel, and spending on voter outreach programs so as not to sacrifice their ability to advertise on television. Consequently, this option would also serve to reduce the amount of personal campaigning and grass-roots political activity conducted by a presidential candidate. A system of private financing modified to reduce the influence of wealthy interests will thus force candidates to place even more emphasis on money and promote the types of campaigns that will only serve to reduce the contact between candidates and voters, and enhance feelings of alienation and powerlessness among the electorate.

Another major disadvantage of private financing is that it would benefit certain types of candidates. In particular, the end of public financing might provide a great advantage to candidates with substantial personal resources, such as H. Ross Perot, who could finance a competitive national effort out of their own pockets. While there are few individuals with Perot's resources, a Perot or similar candidate (recall that in the past decade businessmen Lee Iacocca and Peter Ueberroth have been mentioned as potential candidates) could conceivably outspend the nominees of the two major parties in a race without public funding. At the very least, this sort of candidate could outspend opponents in the crucial early stages of a presidential contest and thus gain a head start in the race for the Oval Office. Individual wealth or, more likely, fundraising ability might also be given greater emphasis by the major parties in assessing potential nominees, since a party's prospects might be enhanced by a candidate with proven fundraising power. This, despite the fact that an ability to raise money is a poor basis for considering an individual as a possible candidate for the nation's highest office. Over time, the presidential race might begin to reflect the patterns emerging in other arenas, such as U.S. Senate elections and some local contests (for example, the 1993 Los Angeles mayoral race), where wealthy candidates able to finance their own campaigns are becoming more and more common.

Private financing would also benefit incumbents. As a proven winner, an incumbent president usually runs for reelection with a well-established financial base and without having to face a serious challenge for the nomination. This would be more likely under private financing since challengers could not rely on matching funds to help fuel their bids, as was the case with Democrat Jerry Brown in 1980 and Republican Pat Buchanan in 1992. Consequently, an incumbent president would probably secure his party's nomination before a prospective opponent and thus be able to get a head start on general election fundraising, which could provide a financial lead that proves impossible to overcome. Similarly, in a race without an incumbent, the candidate who wraps up the nomination most quickly would be able to get a head start on fundraising. As a result, there would be a greater likelihood of significant resource gaps or a very uneven "playing field" in presidential election campaigns. This, in turn, might serve to diminish the competitiveness of presidential contests and discourage some potential challengers from entering the race due to their lack of desire to face a well-heeled incumbent or the prospect of having to devote most of their time to raising funds rather than meeting with voters.

Finally, the absence of public subsidies would have a detrimental effect on nomination contests. In general, the system would provide an advantage to better-known and well-established candidates who have proven fundraising support and broad name recognition. These candidates would generally be able to outspend their lesser-known opponents by significant margins and these underdogs would not have access to public subsidies to help them generate the funds needed to mount a viable campaign. Nomination contests would thus be less competitive and would offer fewer choices to the electorate. In addition, there would be little incentive for candidates to rely on small donations in the financing of their campaigns. There would be a greater incentive for candidates to solicit large donors who could write a $1,000 check and PAC contributions, which might serve to reduce financial participation in presidential campaigns.

Public financing should not be abolished or allowed to run a course toward financial bankruptcy. Instead, Congress should reform the system to build upon its present strengths and correct the faults revealed in recent elections. To achieve this end, legislators must do more than address the program's financial problems. They must also make some changes in the broader structure of the campaign finance system.

REFORMING THE CHECKOFF

The best way to guarantee that the public financing program will have the revenue needed to meet the resource demands of a presidential election is to require by statute that the Treasury provide the sums earned by qualified candidates and parties. Each election cycle, the Treasury would simply make payments to eligible candidates based on the amounts certified by the FEC. Allowing the Treasury to spend funds under general authorizing legislation similar to that used for social security or government medical programs or federal flood insurance would eliminate the need for the checkoff. This would simplify the administration of the system and save the government the expense of processing checkoff designations, which currently costs an estimated $500,000 a year.[2] The drawback to this proposal is that it is politically unrealistic given the current legislative climate and public attitudes. The public's distrust of politicians and the partisan differences over public funding make it highly improbable that Congress would adopt an "entitlement" program for presidential candidates. The most pragmatic approach to reform is therefore to consider other alternatives.

A more politically acceptable solution suggested by former FEC Commissioner Thomas Josefiak and others is to eliminate the checkoff and fund the system through the appropriations process, which is the way Congress finances most other government programs. According to Josefiak, this approach would end the "fiction" of the checkoff, which "involves no donation by the taxpayer" and is "merely an expression of taxpayer consent for the government to spend funds for a particular purpose."[3] This change would also save the money spent annually by the IRS to process checkoff designations.

The problem with this solution is demonstrated by the experience in Florida, which adopted a similar approach when it established a partial program of public finance for statewide elections in 1986. Because the state lacks an income tax, the program had to be funded through annual appropriations and fines paid by those found guilty of violating election laws. When this law was first enacted, the state legislature set aside funds as a first installment toward payment of the costs of the 1990 election. Budget problems then led the legislature to rescind the appropriation a few months later, and no additional funds were appropriated before the 1990 contests.[4]

To make public funding dependent on the appropriations process would make program revenues less secure than they are at present. With each election cycle, presidential campaign strategies would become dependent on congressional decision-making, shifting public and partisan preferences, and competing budget priorities. Candidates might have a much more difficult time planning their campaigns since the final vote on an appropriation bill would usually not take place before the time when most candidates make their decision to run. In addition, unless a multi-year appropriation was adopted, Congress would have to approve funding three times in each election cycle because public monies are usually distributed in three different fiscal years: convention funds are released in the late summer of the pre-election year (fiscal year A), general election funds are released in the election year (fiscal year B), and matching funds are paid during the primaries (fiscal year B) and thereafter, including the period after the election if candidates are eligible for subsidies to help them resolve their debts (fiscal year C). Candidates could therefore conceivably enter the race expecting to receive public subsidies only to find out after they had begun to campaign that the level of funding they expected had not been approved.

The most pragmatic means of meeting the revenue needs of the public funding program is to revise the current income tax checkoff. Most importantly, the structural flaw in the program should be corrected by indexing the amount that a taxpayer can designate to the Presidential Election Campaign Fund. This will ensure that contributions correspond to payments, which are indexed under the current law. Specifically, the income tax checkoff should be adjusted when inflation warrants an increase of a full dollar, rounded to the nearest dollar. This will preclude the need for annual changes and prevent the IRS from having to establish absurdly precise amounts. If this proposal is implemented for the 1994 tax returns, or applied retroactively to these returns, it will generate enough revenue to finance future elections and place the program on solid financial footing in the years ahead.

Besides adjusting the checkoff, Congress should consider changing the eligibility requirements. Public financing is the lone historical example of a federal program that has the size of its appropriation essentially determined by the express consent of the taxpayers. This principle of consent stems from the original idea behind public financing, which was to create a funding scheme for presidential elections based on the principle of "one person, one vote." In accordance with this principle, all tax filers should be allowed to participate and make a contribution to the Fund.

The present system is based on the notion that an individual who pays taxes should have an opportunity to decide whether to designate a dollar to public funding. Consequently, almost one out of five tax filers is disenfranchised from the system because he or she has no tax liability. While a few members of Congress raised this issue when the idea of a checkoff was originally proposed, this issue raised little concern and drew scant attention. The primary consideration of the authors of the checkoff was whether this mechanism would provide the revenue needed to reimburse the parties for the costs of the presidential campaign and its advantages vis-a-vis the tax deduction for political contributions proposed by the Johnson administration. Although no detailed analyses were conducted, legislators took an "educated guess" that the checkoff would provide adequate revenues, given the number of taxpayers eligible to participate, and that this approach would be less costly than other reforms being proposed.[5]Accordingly, the checkoff was adopted without having to confront the issue of eligibility.

Under the current system, individuals may be eligible one year and ineligible the next simply because of changes in their income or tax status. Since those who are eligible experience no change in their liability or refund by virtue of participation, it is difficult to see why those without any liability in a particular year should be excluded from the process. The current approach is also hard to justify in that an individual who is ineligible to contribute to the Fund could receive payments from the Fund if he or she fulfilled the candidate eligibility requirements.

If the eligibility provisions were liberalized, the law would be more effective. Expanded eligibility would promote the basic objective of the checkoff, which is to broaden participation in the financing of campaigns. It would also improve the financial status of the Fund since the available evidence suggests that a significant percentage of those who are currently excluded from the system would be willing to make a contribution.

Action should also be taken to improve the level of public understanding of the checkoff and, more generally, the role of public funding in presidential elections. With each passing election, the number of voters with first-hand knowledge of Watergate and the abuses that led to the adoption of the public financing program declines. Public knowledge of the reforms, which is already inadequate, is thus likely to continue to decline in the future. By initiating a nationwide public education effort, Congress can help to avert this problem and guarantee that taxpayers are making an informed choice when deciding on the checkoff.

Congress should authorize the expenditure of one percent of the annual receipts from the checkoff for public education efforts. These monies, to be administered by the FEC, would be used to conduct an extensive public awareness outreach program designed to explain the purposes of public funding, as well as the operation of the checkoff. This effort, which should be carried out in coordination with the IRS and Department of the Treasury, should build upon the modest program conducted by the FEC in 1990 and 1991. The monies would be used for such purposes as the production and broadcast of public service advertisements, the production of print materials, the purchase of advertising time, and additional research into public attitudes concerning the checkoff and public funding. The information disseminated through the program, however, should do more than highlight the checkoff and explain its tax consequences; it should also describe how the funds are used and the broad objectives of the law. In addition, Congress should instruct the IRS to expand its discussion of the checkoff in tax instructions to clarify the role of the checkoff and the purposes of public funding.

Finally, more information is needed about the activity of the check-off and Presidential Election Campaign Fund if legislators and government agencies are to make informed decisions about public funding in the future. The information currently published by the IRS is completely inadequate for any kind of reasoned analysis of the checkoff program. The IRS should be required to provide a complete summary of checkoff activity for each tax year. This report should include a detailed account of the number of returns filed, the number filed in each checkoff box category, and rates of participation for each checkoff category. It should provide checkoff information on the basis of the number of joint returns and single returns, returns with tax liability and those without, and the different methods of preparation and processing (e.g., self-prepared return, unpaid preparer, paid preparer, and electronic filing). It should also discuss state-by-state participation rates and present the types of statistical summaries that are published for most other lines on federal tax returns.

This information would provide policy makers with the information needed to gain a clear understanding of what is happening with the checkoff and of the changes over time that are affecting participation rates and revenues. Since the IRS already gathers similar data for most other items on the tax form and publishes them in its *Statistics of Income Bulletin* , this task should require minimal additional work for the agency. The IRS should simply compile and report checkoff data as part of its regular summary and analysis of tax information. Since, to date, they have not undertaken this task voluntarily, Congress should mandate such reporting from the agency in the future.

REFORMING THE MATCHING FUNDS PROGRAM

The matching funds program has proven to be one of the most successful components of the public finance system, but a number of revisions are needed to improve the effectiveness of the program and ensure its adaptability to the changing resource demands of presidential nomination campaigns. In general, future changes should adjust the program's thresholds and limits to guard against the unintended consequences of inflation. The program's spending limits should also be revised to reduce the accounting and reporting requirements imposed on campaigns, as well as the incentive to circumvent the law.

One change that makes sense is to adjust the qualifying threshold for matching subsidies to ensure that only those candidates who demonstrate broad support are eligible to receive public money. The current threshold, which requires that a candidate raise $5,000 in each of twenty states in contributions of $250 or less, is increasingly easy to achieve, especially when the effect of inflation is taken into account. Nor is it a particularly stringent standard. The federal financial requirement is less than half that of New York City's public financing program, which requires candidates for mayor to raise $250,000 in order to qualify for subsidies. It is even lower than the requirement for New York City's council president or comptroller candidates, who must raise $125,000.[6]

A more appropriate standard would be one that accounts for inflation and revises the threshold accordingly. The threshold should be increased to about $250,000, with future adjustments based on inflation and rounded to the nearest $50,000 or $100,000 increment. In addition, the number of qualifying states should be increased to at least 25 in order to ensure that candidates receiving public money enjoy a modest breadth of support. Such a standard would ensure that the threshold remains relatively comparable to the original 1974 provision. It would also help to ensure that the law does not serve as an incentive for fringe candidates or other individuals who would decide to run largely because public subsidies were easy to attain. Yet, at the same time, this reform would not result in a mark set so high that lesser-known candidates or minor parties could not qualify.

The payment schedule for matching funds should also be revised to make the program more favorable for candidates. Under current law, the first checks are not released until January 1 of the election year. While candidates can gain earlier access to the sums accrued by securing bank loans against anticipated payments, there should be no need for this practice. Why should a campaign have to undertake additional paperwork and reporting requirements, as well as bank and interest charges, simply to gain access to monies it has earned by right? Changing the date for the commencement of payments to July 1 of the year before the election would allow candidates to gain access to these funds when they are needed most, which is in the earliest stages of a campaign. Matching funds could then be used to defray the start-up costs of a campaign or could serve as "seed money" for raising additional funds. Candidates, especially those who are not well known nationwide, would thus be in a better position to meet the heavy initial costs of the front-loaded delegate selection process.

In order to ensure a consistent flow of public money to deserving candidates, the Treasury Department should repeal the monthly payment schedule it adopted in anticipation of a 1992 shortfall and return to the practice of making payments every two weeks. Although this may seem to be a relatively unimportant change, the delayed payment schedule adopted in 1991, which called for the issuance of matching funds only once a month, created unnecessary complications for many of the 1992 candidates, especially in the more competitive Democratic contest.

Monthly payments served to increase the financial pressures faced by these campaigns and forced most of the candidates to take out loans in January and February to get through the initial stage of primaries. This might not have been necessary if candidates had had access to matching monies on a timely basis.

Another reform that would help to reduce the financial burden placed on candidates is to increase the amount an individual may contribute and the corresponding matching requirement. The $1,000 maximum on individual gifts is yet another aspect of the law that was not adjusted to account for inflation. As a result, the maximum gift now has a relative purchasing power of about $360. Adjusting the contribution limit would raise the maximum gift to about $2,500, which would make it much easier for candidates to amass the sums needed to finance a viable campaign. The amount eligible for matching should also be increased from the first $250 contributed by an individual to the first $500. This would reduce the need to begin fundraising early in the pre-election year, while ensuring that candidates continue to rely on public sources for a significant share of their campaign revenues.

Simply reducing fundraising pressures, however, is not enough to ensure a more effective regulatory system and greater compliance with the law. For these ends to be achieved, reform must also encompass the laws regarding campaign spending. And the most important step to be taken is to abolish the state spending ceilings.

For a number of years, the FEC has urged Congress to eliminate the caps on state expenditures in primary campaigns. The Commission notes that these limits are basically administered for the sole purpose of regulating expenditures in Iowa and New Hampshire because candidates are "unable or do not wish to expend an amount equal to the limitation" in any other state.[7] The law thus imposes a significant administrative burden on candidates and the FEC in an effort to check spending in only two states. Furthermore, experience has shown that these caps are no longer needed to address the primary concerns that led to their adoption. State ceilings were established in part to discourage candidates from placing heavy reliance on the outcome of large state primaries. Legislators were concerned that candidates would concentrate their spending in large delegate-rich states as a way of securing their party's nomination.[8] Large-state spending, however, has not been an issue since the FECA was adopted in 1974. This is largely due to party rules reforms that have taken place since 1974, which make it highly unlikely that a candidate could win the nomination by pursuing a large-state strategy or even a regional strategy barring some extraordinary circumstance.

State ceilings were also predicated on the assumption that the best way to improve competition is to restrict the spending of well-financed candidates, even though there is no clear evidence that state spending determines primary outcomes.[9] The experience with state limits suggests that a more effective and practical way to improve competition may be to ensure that all candidates have a fair opportunity to raise the funds needed to wage a viable campaign. Instead of narrowly restricting expenditures in an effort to impose a "level playing field" on an inherently unequal game, the law should allow relatively unknown challengers to raise the sums needed to launch a campaign and contest the early primaries. This objective can be accomplished through changes in the matching funds program and contribution limits.

Finally, the FEC's new regulations have stripped the state ceilings of any effect they might have and turned them into little more than an accounting exercise. Congress should now recognize the failure of this experiment and ease the accounting requirements of the law further by abolishing the state limits. At the same time, the exemption contained within the law for fundraising expenditures should be abolished and the 20 percent allocation for such costs incorporated into one aggregate national spending ceiling. This will also help to alleviate the accounting and reporting requirements of the law, while still ensuring full public disclosure of all spending. These changes will also reduce the FEC's auditing workload, which will help speed up the auditing process and allow these overseers to concentrate on more important potential violations of the law.

Some supporters of public financing have also advocated the elimination of the national spending cap and the adoption of an approach commonly characterized as "floors without ceilings." Under this proposal, candidates would continue to receive public subsidies in order to ensure that they would have the revenues needed to spread their messages to voters, but the subsidy would be granted with no spending strings attached. The rationale for this approach is best described as follows:

> This concept [floors without ceilings] is favored by many of the mature democracies in Western Europe; the idea is that partial public funding, or a floor, gives candidates (or in Western Europe, parties) at least minimal access to the electorate and provides alternative funds so that candidates (or parties) can reject undesirable private contributions. If this approach were accepted by the Congress, the absence of spending limits would avoid the constitutional issues raised in the *Buckley* case. Although this system appears to favor incumbents who have an advantage in raising funds, the floors actually assist challengers by providing them with money, thereby giving them some degree of access to the voting public.[10]

This reform certainly deserves consideration, especially insofar as this system would be the most workable regulatory approach since it would eliminate most of the restraints imposed on candidates and would be easy to administer.

There are a few reasons, however, why the national cap should be retained. First, in past elections, few candidates have come close to the national limit. Those who did have in every instance slowed their spending toward the end of the campaign in recognition of the aggregate ceiling. The law has thus had some effect, albeit a relatively minor one, on restricting spending, especially for those candidates who have emerged as the party nominee.

Second, the national ceiling plays a role in guarding against the sort of excessive spending on the part of a candidate that may result in an unfair advantage in the general election. For example, in 1984, Ronald Reagan might have spent millions of dollars more during the primary period were it not for the overall cap. Since he was not seriously challenged for the nomination, he did not need to wage an intensive primary campaign. Yet, he spent the maximum amount allowed under the law, including the maximum fundraising allowance, prior to being officially renominated. Most of this spending was devoted to shoring up his political support and laying the groundwork for his general election campaign.[11] Without a national cap, a candidate in a similar situation could engage in unlimited spending and might establish a lead so great that the general election would be no contest at all. An aggregate ceiling thus reduces the possibility of a candidate achieving an unfair advantage by virtue of excessive spending.

Third, without state ceilings, candidates will have broad discretion to shape their spending strategies as they see fit, but they will not be able to engage in a virtual "spending arms race" in the guise of a nomination contest. The national cap thus helps to minimize inordinate spending or the influence of an extremely wealthy candidate who might seek to win the nomination by simply outspending all opponents. While such spending would certainly not guarantee the nomination (after all, in 1980 Republican John Connally spent $12 million but earned the support of only one delegate), it would contribute to perceptions that the presidency is "up for sale" or that only those with big money "have a chance," which would intensify the level of public cynicism and alienation.

Of course, these arguments do not deny the fact that candidates under the current system may spend amounts far in excess of the national limit. The law, however, at least imposes penalties for such blatant violations and the potential political consequences of such an action must be taken into account by any candidate who considers such an action. In addition, a revised system, as has been noted, would help to reduce the incentive to pursue this practice. Although the current system is far from perfect, it is an improvement over a system without any form of restraint.

The best approach to reform of the national limit might therefore be to increase the ceiling so that it better reflects the actual rise in the costs of the goods and services that form the core of a presidential campaign. Although there is no precise index for determining the growth in the costs of such services, a reasonable possibility might be to increase the amount a candidate may legally spend from the $33.1 million level established for the 1992 election to a 1992 base amount of about $40 million with future adjustments for inflation. This higher limit would provide those few candidates who reach the limit, especially those engaged in a competitive nomination contest, with greater flexibility in meeting the actual costs of a campaign. Although this solution may not be the ultimate answer to the problems of spending limits, it should help to reduce the incentive to circumvent the law and guard against inordinate spending in the absence of a more suitable alternative.

REFORMING THE SOFT MONEY SYSTEM

No reform of the campaign finance system can be considered successful if it fails to address the problems created by the rise of soft money in general election campaigns. Soft money has been the focal point of most of the criticisms leveled against the FECA in recent years and many observers have advocated an outright ban on this source of funding. It is important to note, however, that soft money has certain merits in addition to its problems. Most importantly, it permits party organizations to participate in national electoral campaigns. Future reform in this area should therefore not eliminate soft money altogether, but instead prevent the abuses that have occurred in the past while retaining some means for national party organizations to play a role in presidential elections. That is, proposals for reform should balance the need to strengthen the role of parties in the political system with the need to provide full disclosure and protect against any possible undue influence on the part of large donors.

The first step that must be taken in order to improve the present system is to ensure that all soft money transactions are subject to full disclosure. The FEC now requires national party committees to report all receipts and disbursements made from party accounts, whether or not they are connected to federal election activity. The Commission also requires that contributions and allocations from nonfederal funds be disclosed. These changes constitute an important first step in addressing the issues raised by soft money financing. Significant sums of money, however, remain hidden from public view. The law needs to be strengthened to ensure that a complete accounting of party activity is made available to the public.

Federal law should also require a detailed accounting of all soft money transactions. Besides reporting the amount and source of each donation and the accounts into which it was deposited, the committees should also disclose the details of any transfers made between accounts. The disclosure reports filed in 1992 under the FEC regulations show hundreds of thousands of dollars at a time being shifted around with the only description noted as "interfund transfer." Such scant information makes it impossible to trace the flow of nonfederal funds in the political system. Any transfers made between party accounts should include a specific itemization of the reason for the transfer. While these provisions will increase the reporting burden imposed on national party organizations, they are needed to provide a clear understanding of the flow of nonfederal funds at the federal level and to prevent any inappropriate commingling of nonfederal and federal monies.

Another way to improve disclosure is to require state and local committees to report the amounts and purposes of any contributions and disbursements made from accounts maintained by state party organizations. Under the current rules, national committees are required to report the amounts transferred to state and local party organs, and these committees report monies raised and spent in support of federal candidates. Other sums raised by state and local committees can only be determined, at best, by reviewing state disclosure records. Given the efficacy of these laws, the use of these funds essentially remains a mystery. While it is important to respect state authority and the principle of federalism, federal law could require state and local committees to disclose all disbursements for such activities as voter registration drives, voter identification and mobilization programs, polling, and generic advertising, since these efforts may influence federal elections. This would provide more knowledge of the role of soft money in national elections and of the extent to which nonfederal funds are used to assist federal candidates.

The second step needed to clean up soft money is to place limits on the sources and size of contributions to national party accounts. Generally, reform should follow a path designed to turn soft money into hard money; that is, to bring contributions for nonfederal or grass-roots activity into the purview of federal regulation and limit these donations. Most importantly, federal law should ban any contributions made by corporations or drawn from labor union treasury funds. These two sources of contributions have long been prohibited in federal campaigns and, even though the funds are not directly given to candidates, should be banned as a vehicle for backdoor financing. Prohibiting contributions from these sources is in keeping with the original spirit of the earliest federal campaign finance laws and will help to diminish popular perceptions of the role of special interests in national campaigns.

Individual contributions to nonfederal accounts should also be limited. In this regard, one proposal worth consideration is an idea suggested by the Clinton administration, which calls for the creation of a new contribution category—donations for grass-roots political activities.[12] Under current law, an individual is allowed to give a total of $25,000 to federal candidates and parties each year, or $50,000 for each two-year election cycle. The maximum amount an individual can give to a candidate is $1,000 per election and, to a party, $20,000 a year. The administration's proposal would increase the two-year maximum to $60,000. Within that limit, an individual can donate up to $25,000 to candidates, $20,000 to the national party committees, and up to $20,000 to a party for grass-roots political activities in the states. The proposal thus limits the amount an individual can give for the types of activities exempted under the FECA's soft money provisions. Because the total amount represented in the three categories exceeds the maximum amount an individual may contribute, donors will have to choose how to distribute their funds among these broad purposes and establish their own priorities.

The merits of this plan are that it limits the size and sources of contributions, while allowing the national committees to maintain a role in the financing of national elections. An individual would be allowed to give no more than $40,000 to a national party committee for the financing of grass-roots or nonfederal activities in each election cycle. The plan thus eliminates the large, unrestricted soft money gifts that have raised so much concern in recent elections. The national committee would also no longer be able to accept huge corporate gifts or labor union donations. At the same time, the contribution level is set high enough so that parties will be able to raise sufficient funds to finance voter outreach programs, provide limited services to party subsidiaries and candidates, and make contributions to those seeking office at the state and local level. While some may question the particulars of this approach, the basic notion meets the broad criteria that should ground any future reform: it preserves a meaningful role for party organizations in national elections and eliminates large donations from wealthy interests.

The major shortcoming of this proposal is its failure to prevent wealthy interests from making large soft money contributions. Since state laws would still allow such donations, contributors could still give large sums for grass-roots activities by making these contributions directly to the state parties. This possibility highlights the problem of relying on federal statutes to regulate activity in a party system grounded on the principle of federalism. In order to eliminate the role of large contributors from the political system, federal reform is not enough. Reform is also needed at the state level, especially in those states that still allow unlimited political donations and contributions from corporations and labor unions.

As the Center for Responsive Politics has suggested, there is a need for uniform campaign finance codes at the state level, similar to the Uniform Commercial Code that was established some years ago to standardize state approaches to regulating commercial transactions.[13] Toward this end, the Council on Governmental Ethics Laws has drafted a model campaign finance statute for use as a guide to help states frame new legislation.[14] While state legislatures are making progress in this area (in 1991 alone ten states passed new laws establishing or reducing campaign contribution limits), more needs to be done before these fat cat contributions are cleansed from the political system.

As long as state laws allow unlimited corporate and individual gifts, national party staff or campaign personnel could conceivably circumvent any federally imposed limits on soft money by soliciting large gifts that would violate federal law and directing them to state committees. For example, national party fundraisers could ask wealthy contributors to send a contribution of $100,000 or more directly to a particular state party account without the donation ever being deposited in a national party's bank account. To minimize this possibility, federal regulations should ban the solicitation of such gifts. Congress should adopt provisions similar to those that have been drafted for independent expenditures, which would prohibit any federal candidate, campaign staff member, party staff member, fundraiser, or other agent from soliciting, commanding, influencing, or controlling contributions made directly to state parties. In addition, Congress should establish a provision similar to that contained in Senate bill S. 3, which was adopted by the Senate in 1993 and prohibits any federal candidate or office-holder from raising or spending any funds in connection with a federal, state, or local election, including funds for registration and get-out-the-vote drives and generic advertising, unless the funds are raised in accordance with federal law.[15]

Another provision of S. 3 that should be incorporated into federal regulations is a limitation on the amount a party may spend on exempted grass-roots activities. Instead of the unrestricted spending allowed under current law, the bill establishes a limit of four cents times the voting age population of a state on all spending by state and local party committees in connection with a presidential general election campaign.[16] This new coordinated expenditure allowance, which is imposed on all expenditures other than generic television advertising, would supplement the current limit on national party coordinated spending. Had this

provision been in place for the 1992 election cycle, it would have
restricted soft money expenditures, excluding television advertising, to
a total of $20.6 million per party.

A ceiling on grass-roots spending would guard against excessive spending in a particular state and encourage national party committees to distribute grass-roots funds more evenly among the states. It would also force
state and local party committees within a state to work together more
closely to plan spending strategies and establish financial priorities.
So, despite limiting party spending to a certain extent, this reform will
not only provide party organizations with the funds needed to conduct
extensive voter registration and turnout drives, but will also serve to enhance
the role of the national committees as financial brokers and active participants in the development of general election strategies. This change
may also help to broaden participation in the planning and implementation of such programs, and encourage stronger working rela-
tionships between national and state party organizations.

On balance, public financing represents a great improvement in the
financing of presidential campaigns. The system, however, does have major
flaws. This is not unexpected. Indeed, it would be unrealistic to expect
that so ambitious a project would not be characterized by some major
problems given the dynamic nature of the electoral process and the likelihood of unintended consequences that affect almost all regulatory programs. As with most legislative initiatives, the success of public funding
depends in large part on the ability of policy makers to amend the law
in response to changing circumstances. But it has now been more than
a decade since Congress has revised the rules governing the public
funding program. The need for change is now compelling. If Congress
takes up this task, public financing should prove to be even more beneficial in the future and legislators will be able to extend this reform to
other electoral arenas with greater confidence and authority.

APPENDIXES

APPENDIX 1

MAJOR PARTY PRESIDENTIAL CAMPAIGN EXPENDITURE LIMITS AND PUBLIC FUNDING: 1976–1992

($ MILLIONS)

Year	Prenomination Campaign			Nominating Convention	General Election Campaign		
	National Spending Limit[a]	Exempt Fund Raising[b]	Overall Spending Limit[c]	Convention Grant[d]	Public Treasury Grant[e]	National Party Spending Limit[f]	Overall Spending Limit[g]
1976	10.9 +	2.2 =	3.1	2.2	21.8 +	3.2 =	25.0
1980	14.7 +	2.9 =	7.7	4.4	29.4 +	4.6 =	34.0
1984	20.2 +	4.0 =	24.2	8.1	40.4 +	6.9 =	47.3
1988	23.1 +	4.6 =	27.7	9.2	46.1 +	8.3 =	54.4
1992	27.6 +	5.5 =	33.1	11.0	55.2 +	10.3 =	65.5

[a] Based on $10 million plus cost-of-living increases (COLA) using 1974 as the base year. Eligible candidates may receive no more than one-half the national spending limit in public matching funds. To become eligible candidates must raise $5,000 in private contributions of $250 or less in each of twenty states. The federal government matches each contribution to qualified candidates up to $250. Publicly funded candidates also must observe spending limits in the individual states equal to the greater of $200,000 + COLA (base year 1974), or $1.6 x the voting-age population (VAP) of the state + COLA.

b Candidates may spend up to 20 percent of the national spending limit for fund raising.

c Legal and accounting expenses to insure compliance with the law are exempt from the spending limit.

d Based on $2 million + COLA (base year 1974). Under the 1979 FECA Amendments, the basic grant was raised to $3 million. In 1984, Congress raised the basic grant to $4 million.

e Based on $20 million + COLA (base year 1974).

f Based on $.02 x VAP of the United States + COLA.

g Compliance costs are exempt from the spending limit.

Source: Herbert Alexander, "Administering the U.S. Tax Check-Off," *Journal of Behavioral and Social Sciences* 37 (1992) and Federal Election Commission, *Record* 18 (March 1992).

APPENDIX 2A

PUBLIC FINANCING: 1992 ELECTION

Candidates/ Committee	Original Amount Certified ($)	Repayment to Date ($)	Net Public Money to Date ($)
Primary			
Larry Agran (D)	269,691.68	0.00	269,691.68
Jerry Brown (D)	4,239,404.83	97,673.96	4,141,730.87
Pat Buchanan (R)	5,199,987.25	0.00	5,199,987.25
George Bush (R)	10,658,520.94	0.00	10,658,520.94
Bill Clinton (D)	12,536,135.4	0.00	12,536,135.47
Lenora Fulani (NA)	2,013,323.42	0.00	2,013,323.42
John Hagelin (NLP)	353,159.89	0.00	353,159.89
Tom Harkin (D)	2,103,361.85	0.00	2,103,361.85
Bob Kerrey (D)	2,195,529.81	0.00	2,195,529.81
Paul Tsongas (D)	2,995,449.27	0.00	2,995,449.27
Doug Wilder (D)	289,026.67	0.00	289,026.67
Total Primary	42,853,591.08	97,673.96	42,755,917.12
Convention			
Democratic	11,048,000.00	0.00	11,048,000.00
Republican	11,048,000.00	0.00	11,048,000.00
Total Convention	22,096,000.00	0.00	22,096,000.00
General			
George Bush R)	55,240,000.00	0.00	55,240,000.00
Bill Clinton (D)	55,240,000.00	0.00	55,240,000.00
Total General	110,480,000.00	0.00	110,480,000.00
Grand Total	175,429,591.08	97,673.96	175,331,917.12

Note: Repayments from the general election and convention committees are not returned to the Presidential Election Campaign Fund.

Source: Federal Election Commission.

PUBLIC FINANCING: 1988 ELECTION

Candidates/ Committee	Original Amount Certified ($)	Repayment to Date ($)	Net Public Money to Date ($)
Primary			
Bruce Babbitt (D)	1,078,939.44	1,004.80	1,077,934.64
George Bush (R)	8,393,098.56	113,079.70	8,280,018.86
Robert Dole (R)	7,618,115.99	235,821.53	7,382,294.46
Michael Dukakis (D)	9,040,028.33	485,000.00	8,555,028.33
Pete Dupont (R)	2,550,954.18	25,775.49	2,525,178.69
Lenora Fulani (NA)	938,798.45	16,692.11	922,106.34
Richard Gephardt (D)	3,396,276.37	121,572.28	3,274,704.09
Albert Gore, Jr. (D)	3,853,401.56	4,327.41	3,849,074.15
Alexander Haig (R)	538,539.20	8,834.14	529,705.06
Gary Hart (D)	1,124,708.0	38,215.79	1,086,492.30
Jesse Jackson (D)	8,021,707.31	75,000.00	7,946,707.31
Jack Kemp (R)	5,984,773.65	103,555.03	5,881,218.62
Lyndon LaRouche (D)	825,576.99	4,795.32	820,781.67
Pat Robertson (R)	10,410,984.83	0.00	10,410,984.83
Paul Simon (D)	3,774,344.7	0.00	3,774,344.77
Total Primary	67,550,247.72	1,233,673.60	66,316,574.12
Convention			
Democratic	9,220,000.00	57,294.06	9,162,705.94
Republican	9,220,000.00	32,506.57	9,187,493.43
Total Convention	18,440,000.00	89,800.63	18,350,199.37
General			
George Bush (R)	46,100,000.00	134,834.71	45,965,165.29
Michael Dukakis (D)	46,100,000.00	334,683.20	45,765,316.80
Total General	92,200,000.00	469,517.91	91,730,482.09
Grand Total	178,190,247.72	1,792,992.14	176,397,255.58

Note: Repayments from the general election and convention committees are not returned to the Presidential Election Campaign Fund.

Source: Federal Election Commission.

APPENDIX 2C

PUBLIC FINANCING: 1984 ELECTION

Candidates/ Committee	Original Amount Certified ($)	Repayment to Date ($)	Net Public Money to Date ($)
Primary			
Reubin Askew (D)	976,179.04	5,073.55	971,105.49
Alan Cranston (D)	2,113,736.44	26,539.56	2,087,196.88
John Glenn (D)	3,325,382.66	76,146.29	3,249,236.37
Gary Hart (D)	5,333,785.31	1,295.52	5,332,489.79
Ernest Hollings (D)	821,599.85	15,605.59	805,994.26
Jesse Jackson (D)	3,053,185.40	4,538.50	3,048,646.90
Sonia Johnson (C)	193,734.83	0.00	193,734.83
Lyndon LaRouche (D)	494,145.59	0.00	494,145.59
George McGovern (D)	612,734.78	67,726.51	545,088.27
Walter Mondale (D)	9,494,920.93	290,140.55	9,204,780.38
Ronald Reagan (R)	10,100,000.00	403,086.49	9,696,913.51
Total Primary	36,519,404.83	890,152.56	35,629,252.77
Convention			
Democratic	8,080,000.00	20,654.60	8,059,345.40
Republican	8,080,000.00	306,454.29	7,773,545.71
Total Convention	16,160,000.00	327,108.89	15,823,891.11
General			
Walter Mondale (D)	40,400,000.00	181,945.30	40,218,054.70
Ronald Reagan (R)	40,400,000.00	277,244.82	40,122,755.18
Total General	80,800,000.00	459,190.12	80,340,809.88
Grand Total	133,479,404.83	1,676,451.57	131,802,953.26

Note: Repayments from the general election and convention committees are not returned to the Presidential Election Campaign Fund.

Source: Federal Election Commission.

APPENDIX 2D

PUBLIC FINANCING: 1980 ELECTION

Candidates/ Committee	Original Amount Certified ($)	Repayment to Date ($)	Net Public Money to Date ($)
Primary			
John Anderson (I)	2,733,077.02	412,267.54	2,320,809.48
Howard Baker, Jr. (R)	2,635,042.60	104,074.58	2,530,968.02
Edmund Brown, Jr. (D)	892,249.14	18,980.02	873,269.12
George Bush (R)	5,716,246.56	39,691.01	5,676,555.55
Jimmy Carter (D)	5,117,854.45	111,431.13	5,006,423.32
Philip Crane (R)	1,899,631.74	468.00	1,899,163.74
Robert Dole (R)	446,226.09	3,369.44	442,856.65
Edward Kennedy (D)	4,134,815.72	18,534.17	4,116,281.55
Lyndon LaRouche (D)	526,253.19	55,751.45	470,501.74
Ronald Reagan (R)	7,330,262.78	1,052,647.87	6,277,614.91
Total Primary	31,431,659.29	1,817,215.21	29,614,444.08
Convention			
Democratic	4,416,000.00	723,473.24	3,683,526.76
Republican	4,416,000.00	21,395.44	4,394,604.56
Total Covention	8,832,000.00	753,868.68	8,078,131.32
General			
John Anderson (I)	424,304.00	48,786.01	4,193,517.99
Jimmy Carter (D)	29,440,000.00	87,232.02	29,352,767.98
Ronald Reagan (R)	29,440,000.00	279,278.95	29,160,721.05
Total General	63,122,304.00	415,296.98	62,707,007.02
Grand Total	103,385,963.29	2,986,380.87	100,399,582.42

Note: Repayments from the general election and convention committees are not returned to the Presidential Election Campaign Fund.

Source: Federal Election Commission.

APPENDIX 2E

PUBLIC FINANCING: 1976 ELECTION

Candidates/ Committee	Original Amount Certified ($)	Repayment to Date ($)	Net Public Money to Date ($)
Primary			
Birch Bayh (D)	545,710.39	0.00	545,710.39
Lloyd Bentsen (D)	511,022.61	0.00	511,022.61
Jerry Brown (D)	600,203.54	306.00	599,897.54
Jimmy Carter (D)	3,886,465.62	132,387.60	3,754,078.02
Frank Church (D)	640,668.54	0.00	640,668.54
Gerald Ford (R)	4,657,007.82	148,140.41	4,508,867.41
Fred Harris (D)	639,012.53	7,798.32	631,214.21
Henry Jackson (D)	1,980,554.95	17,603.78	1,962,951.17
Ellen McCormack (D)	247,220.37	0.00	247,220.37
Ronald Reagan (R)	5,008,910.66	611,141.89	4,477,768.77
Terry Sanford (D)	246,388.32	48.04	246,340.28
Milton Sharp (D)	299,066.21	299,066.21	0.00
Sargent Shriver (D)	295,711.74	1,553.00	294,158.74
Morris Udall (D)	2,020,257.95	43,113.28	1,977,144.67
George Wallace (D)	3,291,308.81	45,380.98	3,245,927.83
Total Primary	24,949,510.06	1,306,539.51	23,642,970.55
Convention			
Democratic	2,185,829.73	170,093.06	2,015,736.67
Republican	1,963,800.00	382,205.36	1,581,594.64
Total Covention	4,149,629.73	552,298.42	3,597,331.31
General			
Jimmy Carter (D)	21,820,000.00	57,762.21	21,762,237.79
Gerald Ford (R)	21,820,000.00	44,655.00	21,775,345.00
Total General	43,640,000.00	102,417.21	43,537,582.79
Grand Total	72,739,139.79	1,961,255.14	70,777,884.65

Note: Repayments from the general election and convention committees are not returned to the Presidential Election Campaign Fund.

Source: Federal Election Commission.

NOTES

INTRODUCTION

1. FEC, *Report on the Presidential Public Funding Program* (Washington, D.C., April 1993), p. 8.

2. "Press Conference Statement by Joan D. Aikens, Chair, Federal Election Commission," FEC Press Release, December 14, 1992, p. 3.

3. "Campaign Checkoff: Thumbs Are Down," *Boston Globe*, July 29, 1993, p. 19.

4. The FECA of 1971 (Public Law 92-225) was signed into law by President Nixon on February 7, 1972, and went into effect sixty days later. The text of the act is at 86 Stat. 3. For the 1974 amendments (Public Law 93-443), see 88 Stat. 1263; for the 1976 amendments (Public Law 94-283), 90 Stat. 475; and for the 1979 amendments (Public Law 96-187), 93 Stat. 1339.

5. Congressional Quarterly, *Dollar Politics*, 3d ed. (Washington, D.C.: Congressional Quarterly, 1982), p. 8.

6. Herbert Alexander, *Financing Politics*, 3d ed. (Washington, D.C.: Congressional Quarterly, 1984), p. 7.

7. Herbert Alexander, *Financing Politics*, 1st ed. (Washington, D.C.: Congressional Quarterly, 1976), p. 8.

8. See Herbert Alexander, *Financing the 1972 Election* (Lexington, Mass.: Lexington Books, 1976), pp. 39–75 and 513–557.

9. FEC, *Legislative History of the Federal Election Campaign Act Amendments of 1974* (Washington, D.C.: GPO, 1977), p. 107.

10. Public Law 98-355.

11. 26 U.S.C. 9033(c)(1)(B).

12. For example, if each of the major parties, the Democrats and the Republicans, received 40 percent of the vote in an election and a minor party candidate received

10 percent of the vote, the minor party's share (10 percent) compared to the average for the major parties (40 percent) would be one-quarter, or 25 percent. The minor party would thus qualify for 25 percent of the amount allowed by the spending limit.

13. 26 U.S.C. 9008(a).

14. Public Law 92-178. For a discussion of the law, see Joseph E. Cantor, *The Presidential Election Campaign Fund and Tax Checkoff* (Washington, D.C.: Congressional Research Service, 1985).

15. Robert E. Mutch, cited in Glen Craney, "Public Cash for Presidential Bids Could Be In Jeopardy," *Congressional Quarterly Weekly Report*, September 9, 1989, p. 2326.

16. Long's original proposal, S. 3496, was introduced in the 89th Congress on June 15, 1966. For a discussion of the bill, see Long's remarks in *Congressional Record*, June 14, 1966, pp. 13123–13124, and U.S. Senate, *Financing Political Campaigns*, Hearings before the Committee on Finance, 89th Cong., 2d sess., August 18 and 19, 1966.

17. *Congressional Record*, June 30, 1966, p. 14862.

18. See U.S. Senate, Committee on Finance, *Foreign Investors Tax Act of 1966; Presidential Election Campaign Fund Act; and Other Amendments*, Senate Report No. 1707, October 11, 1966.

19. See *Financing Political Campaigns*, pp. 38–39 and 47.

20. *Congressional Record*, October 12, 1966, p. 26399.

21. *Buckley v. Valeo*, 424 U.S. 1 (1976). In this opinion, the Court reviews the legislative intent of the FECA. These objectives are also summarized in the FEC's *Report on the Presidential Public Funding Program*, 53–56. For a more detailed legislative history, see Robert E. Mutch, *Campaigns, Congress, and Courts* (New York: Praeger, 1988).

22. Representative Al Swift, *Presidential Election Campaign Fund*, Hearings before the Subcommittee on Elections, Committee on House Administration, 102d Cong., 1st sess., May 1, 1991, p.2.

23. Statement of Dr. Susan S. Lederman in Ibid., p. 83.

24. Senator Mitch McConnell, "No: Public Financing is Not a Desirable Policy," in *Controversial Issues in Presidential Selection*, ed. by Gary L. Rose (Albany, NY: State University of New York Press, 1991), p. 169.

25. Representative Bob Livingston (R-LA), *Congressional Record*, October 29, 1991, p. H8633.

CHAPTER ONE

1. John Warren McGarry, Testimony before the Department of the Treasury, Internal Revenue Service, February 11, 1991, p. 9. A copy of this statement is available from the FEC.

2. The regulations were adopted by the Department of the Treasury on May

10, 1991, and the FEC passed conforming regulations on July 18, 1991. The regulations can be found at 56 *Federal Register* 91 (May 10, 1991), pp. 21596–21600. For a discussion, see FEC, *Record* 17:7 (July 1991), pp. 1–3.

3. FEC, *Annual Report 1990* (Washington, D.C., June 1991), p. 3.

4. FEC, *Annual Report 1992* (Washington, D.C., June 1993), p. 3. The FEC originally projected a $2 million decrease in tax checkoff revenues, based on the anticipated decline in receipts that had occurred in every other election under the public financing program. Yet receipts only declined by about $140,000 in 1991. Receipts in 1992, however, fell about $2.7 million compared to 1991.

5. Based on the estimates presented by FEC Chair Joan D. Aikens in a statement released at a press conference on December 14, 1992. A copy of the statement is available from the FEC.

6. FEC, *Annual Report 1992*, p. 3.

7. "Proposed Testimony and Responses to Questions for Senate Rules Committee, March 6, 1991 Hearing," Memorandum to the Federal Election Commission from John Surina, Staff Director, FEC, February 25, 1991.

8. These figures are based on the national spending limit, which was originally set at $10 million, not the overall limit that includes exempt fundraising costs. For a listing of the specific limits applicable in each election under the act, see Appendix 1.

9. "Proposed Testimony and Responses to Questions for Senate Rules Committee," Response to Questions, p. 1.

10. John Warren McGarry, Statement before the United States Senate Committee on Rules and Administration Regarding the Status of the Presidential Election Campaign Fund, March 6, 1991, p. 8. A copy of this statement is available from the FEC.

11. Representative Bob Livingston, *Congressional Record*, October 29, 1991, p. H8633.

12. See, for example, their respective statements in *Presidential Election Campaign Fund*, Hearings before the Subcommittee on Elections, Committee on House Administration, 102d Cong., 1st sess., May 1, 1991, pp. 77–101.

13. Thomas Schatz, Ibid., p. 62.

14. The FEC does not conduct an independent analysis of tax checkoff activity because this aspect of the program is administered by the IRS. The data available from the FEC on participation in the tax checkoff is obtained from the IRS and is based on the summary of checkoff activity included in the *Annual Report of the IRS Commissioner*. This information is reported in Table 9 of the report and usually presents the results from tax returns of the previous year processed by June of the report year.

15. 26 U.S.C. 6096.

16. Some of these criticisms of the IRS data are also noted in Kim Quaile Hill, "Taxpayer Support for the Presidential Election Campaign Fund," *Social Science Quarterly* 62 (December 1981), p. 768.

17. The usual statistics published by the IRS apparently include only the returns processed by June of the report year. For example, the 1974 and 1975 *Annual Reports of the Commissioner of the IRS* specifically noted that the published figures for the number of returns with designations for the Presidential Election Campaign Fund were based on the individual returns processed between January 1 and June 30 of the report year and that the amount contributed was based on the fiscal year (see the 1974 report, p. 11, and the 1975 report, p. 19). In the 1977 *Annual Report*, the language concerning the time period was dropped and the report noted that the figures were based on the fiscal year. It also noted the rate of participation for the "previous twelve month period," which was slightly higher than the figure reported in 1976 and used by the FEC. Beginning with the 1978 *Annual Report*, the IRS stopped noting the specifications of the time period relevant to the aggregate figures on the checkoff offered in the report. A summary of the annual report data prepared by the IRS Statistics of Income Division entitled, "Presidential Election Campaign Fund Checkoff," notes that the annual report "usually only reports the number of returns processed by June of the report year."

18. A summary of these estimates is available from the FEC. A copy of this summary is in the possession of the author.

19. The complete results of this survey are noted in Table 1.4 below.

20. Hill, "Taxpayer Support for the Presidential Election Campaign Fund," p. 769.

21. Ruth S. Jones and Warren Miller, "Financing Campaigns: Macro Level Innovation and Micro Level Response," *Western Political Quarterly* 38 (June 1985), p. 193.

22. Cited in Jones and Miller, Ibid., p. 193, n. 10. Noragon's findings were presented in a private letter to Jones and Miller. See also, Robert E. Mutch, *Campaigns, Congress, and Courts* (New York: Praeger, 1988), pp. 140–141.

23. Ruth S. Jones, "Contributing as Participation," In *Money, Elections, and Democracy*, ed. by Margaret L. Nugent and John R. Johannes (Boulder, Colo.: Westview Press, 1990), p. 31.

24. The figures in Table 4 represent the final data for the 1988 tax year. Some of the figures differ from those reported by the FEC. This is probably due to the fact that FEC statistics are based on the figures reported in the *Annual Report of the Commissioner of the IRS*, which are usually estimates based on the returns processed as of June of the report year. The amount contributed to the Fund, as noted in Table 1.4, is $31,384,742. This varies slightly from the $32,285,646 reported by the Treasury Department and released by the FEC for the calendar year 1989. This discrepancy may be due to the different time frames employed by the agencies when aggregating data, technical aspects of the administration of the Fund, and time lags in reporting deposits. For example, the Treasury/FEC financial total for 1989 primarily includes receipts from the 1988 tax returns, but also includes late filings from previous tax years and probably some year-end overlap in the transmission of deposits.

25. The analysis in this section assumes that the forms with two boxes checked were joint returns. According to the law, only joint filers may check two boxes. It is possible that this figure also includes some filings by single individuals who did not understand the law or mistakenly checked two boxes.

26. If only 15 percent of the tax returns reported each year since 1989 with a checkoff were filed by ineligible participants and the proportion of one-box to two-box filings returned by these individuals was similar to that of the 1988 tax year, the estimated revenue that would be generated by these filings, if eligible to contribute, is about $16 million, when added to the amount determined for the 1988 tax year. If the percentage of returns filed by ineligible participants is increased to 17 percent, as was the case in the 1988 tax year, the revenue estimate rises to close to $20 million.

27. The data in this paragraph are based on the figures reported in various issues of the IRS's *Statistics of Income Bulletin*. Although different formats have been employed over the years, the figures are reported in Table 1 in the section entitled "Selected Historical and Other Data."

28. See, among others, Raymond Wolfinger and Steven J. Rosenstone, *Who Votes?* (New Haven, Conn.: Yale University Press, 1980), and Steven J. Rosenstone and John Mark Hansen, *Mobilization, Participation, and Democracy in America* (New York: Macmillan, 1993).

29. Quoted in FEC, *Report on the Presidential Public Funding Program* (Washington, D.C., April 1993), p. 74.

30. For a summary of the findings of national polls on campaign finance conducted between January 1980 and December 1990, see Rinn-Sup Shinn, *Campaign Financing: National Public Opinion Polls* (Washington, D.C.: Congressional Research Service, 1991).

31. Frank Sorauf, *Inside Campaign Finance* (New Haven, Conn.: Yale University Press, 1992), p. 146. See also, Frank Sorauf, "Public Opinion on Campaign Finance," in *Money, Elections, Democracy: Reforming Congressional Campaign Finance,* Margaret L. Nugent and John R. Johannes, eds. (Boulder, Colo.: Westview Press, 1990), pp. 207–224.

32. See Ruth S. Jones, "State Public Campaign Finance: Implications for Partisan Politics," *American Journal of Political Science* 25 (May 1981), pp. 342–361, and Jones and Miller, "Financing Campaigns," p. 195.

33. Jones and Miller, "Financing Campaigns," pp. 195–197.

34. Frank Sorauf, *Money in American Elections* (Glenview, Ill.: Scott, Foresman, 1988), p. 219.

35. Paul Raymond, "Determinants of Participation in the Federal Income Tax Checkoff Program," Unpublished manuscript, pp. 11–12.

36. Elizabeth G. King and David G. Wegge, "Determinants of Participation in the Income Tax Check-Off for State Public Funding of Elections," Paper prepared for the 1992 Annual Meeting of the American Political Science Association, September 3–6, 1992, p. 9.

37. Market Decisions Corporation, *Presidential Election Campaign Fund Focus Group Research* (Portland, Oregon: Market Decisions Corporation, 1990).

38. John Warren McGarry, *Presidential Election Campaign Fund*, p. 5.

39. Market Decisions Corporation, *Presidential Election Campaign Fund Focus Group Research*, p. 10.

40. Ibid., p. iv–v.

41. Ibid., p. vi.

42. McGarry, *Presidential Election Campaign Fund*, p. 53, and FEC, *Report on the Presidential Public Funding Program*, p. 75.

43. FEC, *Report on the Presidential Public Funding Program*, pp. 75–76.

44. Based on the usage reported in *Final Report: Federal Election Commission Broadcast Media Public Education Program on the Tax Checkoff* (Washington, D.C.: Washington Independent Productions, 1991).

45. "Tax Checkoff: 'No' by Default," *PACs & Lobbies*, May 15, 1991, p. 10.

46. Interview with Bob Biersack, FEC staff member, May 10 and June 11, 1993.

47. Jones and Miller, "Financing Campaigns," p. 192.

48. Ibid., p. 194.

49. Cited by Fred Wertheimer in *Presidential Election Campaign Fund*, p. 98.

50. Larry Harrington, "Should the Public Funding of Presidential Campaigns Be Abolished?" *Journal of Law and Politics* VIII (Winter 1992), p. 322.

51. Herbert E. Alexander, "Yes: Public Financing is a Desirable Policy," in *Controversial Issues in Presidential Selection*, ed. by Gary L. Rose (Albany, NY: State University of New York Press, 1991), p. 166.

CHAPTER TWO

1. Herbert E. Alexander, "Yes: Public Financing is a Desirable Policy," in *Controversial Issues in Presidential Selection*, ed. by Gary L. Rose (Albany, NY: State University of New York Press, 1991), pp. 159–160.

2. The totals do not include Ellen McCormack, the anti-abortion candidate who ran as a Democrat in 1976, and Lyndon LaRouche, the political extremist who ran as a Democrat in 1980, 1984, and 1988. For the purposes of the analysis in this chapter, these individuals are considered minor candidates.

3. For the specific amounts received by each candidate since 1976, see the tables in Appendix 2.

4. The candidate with the highest percentage of matching funds in each election was: Ellen McCormack, 1976; John Anderson, 1980; Sonia Johnson, 1984; and Lenora Fulani in 1988 and 1992.

5. The candidate with the lowest percentage of matching funds in each election was: Jimmy Carter, 1976; Lyndon LaRouche, 1980, 1984, and 1988; and George Bush in 1992. When LaRouche is excluded, the lowest percentage in 1980 belongs to Carter; in 1984, John Glenn; and in 1988, George Bush.

6. Herbert E. Alexander and Monica Bauer, *Financing the 1988 Election* (Boulder, Colo.: Westview Press, 1991), pp. 22–23.

7. These figures and those in the paragraphs that follow are based on information provided by the FEC on candidate receipts in the 1992 election. The amounts are based on the totals reported as of December 1992.

8. If Brown had received only contributions of $100 or less, 50 percent of his total receipts would have come from matching funds since every contribution would be matchable on a dollar-for-dollar basis. But Brown's campaign also received a loan of $1.2 million and not all of his contributions were matched due to a failure to provide all the necessary information for some contributions and other technical problems with his submissions that are common among all candidate submissions for funds. Usually an average of one to four percent of the contributions submitted for matching are deemed ineligible for various technical reasons.

9. Alexander, "Yes: Public Financing is a Desirable Policy," p. 160.

10. Based on the amount of matching funds received through the February 4, 1992 payments. See FEC, *Record* 18:3 (March 1992), p. 15.

11. FEC, *Reports on Financial Activity, 1983–84, Final Report: Presidential Pre-Nomination Campaigns* (Washington, D.C.: FEC, April 1986), p. 44.

12. FEC, *Record* 14:2 (February 1988), p. 1.

13. Frank Sorauf, *Inside Campaign Finance* (New Haven, Conn.: Yale University Press, 1992), p. 137.

14. 26 U.S.C. 9033(c) and 11 C.F.R. 9033.5.

15. This point was made by Senator Taft in the floor debate on the amendments. His comments are reprinted in FEC, *Legislative History of Federal Election Campaign Act Amendments of 1976* (Washington, D.C.: FEC, 1977), pp. 439–443.

16. 11 C.F.R. 9033.5(b). Since only primaries are considered for purposes of determining eligibility, a candidate can also retain eligibility by choosing to compete only in caucus states.

17. Letter to John McGarry, Chair, FEC, from Gary Sinewski, General Counsel, Fulani for President, December 12, 1991.

18. Memorandum to the Federal Election Commission from Robert J. Costa, FEC Audit Division, May 20, 1992.

19. Memorandum to Robert J. Costa, FEC Audit Division, from Lawrence Noble et al., FEC General Counsel's Office, October 9, 1992.

20. For a more detailed discussion of the changes in the selection process and their effect on the cost of presidential campaigns, see Anthony Corrado, *Creative Campaigning* (Boulder, Colo.: Westview Press, 1992), pp. 26–34.

21. Daniel J. Swillinger, "Reflections on Fifteen Years of Presidential Public Financing," *Journal of Law and Politics* VIII (Winter 1992), p. 340.

22. These figures are based on the amounts reported to the FEC through January 29, 1992.

23. The analysis in this section follows the more extensive discussion in Corrado, *Creative Campaigning*, pp. 34–42.

24. According to one Reagan campaign adviser, the general rule of thumb for estimating the costs of fundraising in the 1980 campaign was $1 for every $4 raised, or 25 percent (Harvard Campaign Finance Study Group, *Financing Presidential Campaigns* [Cambridge, Mass.: Institute of Politics, Harvard University, 1982], pp. 5–22). In the 1990 U.S. Senate races, which are subject to the same contribution limits as presidential elections, the percentage of spending devoted to fundraising averaged about 31 percent (Sara Fritz and Dwight Morris, *Gold-Plated Politics* [Washington, D.C.: Congressional Quarterly, 1992], Table 1–4).

25. Lee Ann Elliott, "Campaign Finance," *Journal of Law and Politics* VIII (Winter 1992), p. 302.

26. See Herbert E. Alexander, *Financing the 1976 Election* (Washington, D.C.: Congressional Quarterly Press, 1979), pp. 308, 314, 322–23, and 328; Herbert E. Alexander, *Financing the 1980 Election* (Lexington, Mass.: Lexington Books, 1983), pp. 172–174; Herbert E. Alexander and Brian A. Haggerty, *Financing the 1984 Election* (Lexington, Mass.: Lexington Books, 1987), p. 165; and Rita Beamish, "GOP Funds Trips as Bush Near Spending Cap," Associated Press Release, July 4, 1988, p. 13.

27. Alexander and Bauer, *Financing the 1988 Election*, p. 18.

28. This percentage is based on the Arbitron ratings for the area of dominant influence (ADI) for the Boston television market.

29. For a detailed account of Reagan's Citizens for the Republic, as well as the activities of other candidate PACs and their role in the presidential selection process, see Corrado, *Creative Campaigning*, Chapters 4–6.

30. In the 1980 election cycle, Republicans Ronald Reagan, George Bush, Robert Dole, and John Connally had PACs; in 1984, Ronald Reagan, and Democrats Walter Mondale, John Glenn, Alan Cranston, and Ernest Hollings; in 1988, Republicans George Bush, Robert Dole, Pierre du Pont, Alexander Haig, Jack Kemp, and Pat Robertson, and Democrats Bruce Babbitt, Joseph Biden, Richard Gephardt, and Paul Simon.

31. See, among others, Brooks Jackson, *Broken Promise: Why the Federal Election Commission Failed* (New York: Priority Press, 1990), and Common Cause, *The Failure-to-Enforce Commission* (Washington, D.C.: Common Cause, 1989).

32. Jackson, *Broken Promise*, pp. 19–20.

33. Letter from John Warren McGarry to U.S. Senator Wendell Ford, March 21, 1991. A copy of this letter is available at the FEC.

34. John Warren McGarry, *Presidential Election Campaign Fund*, Hearings before the Subcommittee on Elections, Committee on House Administration, 102nd Cong., 1st Sess., May 1, 1991, p.17.

35. FEC, *Annual Report 1992*, p. 51.

36. The new regulations are outlined in FEC, *Record* 17 (September 1991), pp. 2–5, and in 56 *Federal Register* 91 (July 29, 1991), pp. 35896–35950.

37. 11 C.F.R. 110.8(c)(2).

38. Based on estimates by the author, calculating the costs of different campaign

budgets for the New Hampshire primary. The high end budget assumes $1.5 million in television time purchased on Boston stations, about $250,000 in television time on Maine and Vermont stations, three early mailings each sent to 200,000 households, and a staff of 100 persons for at least three months.

CHAPTER THREE

1. Candidates are allowed to accept private contributions for separate general election legal and accounting compliance accounts that are used to defray the costs incurred in complying with the law.

2. Herbert E. Alexander, *Financing Politics*, 2nd ed. (Washington, D.C.: Congressional Quarterly Press, 1980), p. 5.

3. The two major party candidates in 1992, Clinton and Bush, received a combined 81 percent of the vote or an average vote share of 40.5 percent. Perot's 19 percent of the votes cast was therefore equal to almost 47 percent of the average major party vote, which would have made him eligible for a subsidy equal to 47 percent of the major party grant of $55.24 million.

4. 11 C.F.R. 102.5(a).

5. Herbert E. Alexander, *"Soft Money" and Campaign Financing* (Washington, D.C.: Public Affairs Council, 1986), p. 5.

6. See United States Senate, *Federal Election Campaign Act Amendments, 1979*, Hearing before the Committee on Rules and Administration, 96th Cong., lst Sess., July 13, 1979, and United States Senate, Committee on Rules and Administration, *Federal Election Campaign Act Amendments of 1979*, Sen. Rpt. 96-319, 96th Cong., 1st Sess., (Washington, D.C.: GPO, 1979).

7. For a list of the specific activities considered exempt under the 1979 law, see 11 C.F.R. 100.7(b)(9), 100.7(b)(15), and 100.7(b)(17).

8. FEC, Advisory Opinions 1978-28 and 1978-50; and 11 C.F.R. 106.1(e), (1980). The initial regulations governing coordinated expenditure allocations are discussed in FEC, *Record, Supplement for State and Local Party Organizations* 6 (August 1980).

9. The regulations can be found in the 55 *Federal Register* 90 (June 26, 1990), pp. 26058-26073. They are discussed in FEC, *Record, Supplement on Allocation* 16 (November 1990).

10. Based on the legislative summaries in *Campaign Finance Law 92: A Summary of State Campaign Finance Laws* (Washington, D.C.: National Clearinghouse on Election Administration, 1992).

11. Corporate contributions have been prohibited in federal election campaigns since the adoption of the Tillman Act in 1907. Contributions from labor union treasury funds were first prohibited under the Smith-Connally Act of 1943. This ban was made permanent by the Taft-Hartley Act of 1947.

12. On the problems of state disclosure laws, see Herbert E. Alexander, *Reform and Reality* (New York: Twentieth Century Fund Press, 1991), pp. 51–71.

13. Alexander, *"Soft Money" and Campaign Financing*, pp. 14–16.

14. Thomas B. Edsall, "The Democrats Will Use the Hard Sell to Pull in the Soft Money," *The Washington Post National Weekly Edition*, July 23, 1984, and Maxwell Glen, "Republicans and Democrats Battling to Raise Big Bucks for Voter Drives," *National Journal*, September 1, 1984, p. 1620.

15. Alexander, *"Soft Money" and Campaign Financing*, pp. 23–24.

16. Ibid., p. 18.

17. Brooks Jackson, "'Soft Money' Givers Named in Reports," *Wall Street Journal*, January 16, 1985.

18. See Ed Zuckerman, "'Soft Money': A New Life for 'Fat Cats'," *PACs & Lobbies*, January 16, 1985, pp. 1–3, and Center for Responsive Politics, *Soft Money—A Loophole for the '80s* (Washington, D.C.: Center for Responsive Politics, 1985).

19. Carol Matlack, "Backdoor Spending," *National Journal*, October 8, 1988, pp. 2516–2517, and Brooks Jackson, "Democrats, Outflanked in Previous Elections, Rival GOP in Financing of Presidential Race," *Wall Street Journal*, October 3, 1988, p. A24.

20. Herbert E. Alexander and Monica Bauer, *Financing the 1988 Election* (Boulder, Colo.: Westview Press, 1991), p. 37. It should be noted that the amounts represented by the number of $100,000 donors exceeds the amounts of soft money reported for each party. This is because the total amount given by a $100,000 contributor is not always in the form of soft money. These donors can give up to $20,000 in hard money to the party under the FECA limits and many do as part of their overall contribution. Some donors may also make contributions directly to state party committees. These gifts are not included in the soft money totals reported by the national committees.

21. Jackson, "Democrats, Outflanked in Previous Elections," p. A24.

22. This figure was reported by a Republican National Committee spokesman and cited in Jean Cobb et al., "All the President's Donors," *Common Cause Magazine* 16 (March/April 1990), p. 23.

23. Jackson, "Democrats, Outflanked in Previous Elections," p. A24.

24. Cobb et al., "All the President's Donors," p. 23.

25. Even these figures do not provide a precise estimate of the amount of soft money raised for the 1992 election. For example, the totals do not include any contributions made directly to state and local parties at the request of national party fundraisers. Nor do they include the soft money donations made in 1989 and 1990 as part of a donor's pledge for the four-year election cycle. They do include all soft money contributions received in 1991 and 1992. Because they are based on a two-year cycle, the amounts may not be directly comparable to the amounts estimated for previous elections.

26. Michael Wines, "Study Finds Money Flowed to Clinton Late in '92," *New York Times*, March 4, 1993, p. A19, and Charles R. Babcock, "Leading GOP Business Donor Gave Democrats Late Help," *Washington Post*, December 9, 1992, p. A21.

27. Common Cause, "Soft Money for President Clinton & Democratic National Committee Tops $29 Million During 1991–92 Election Cycle," Press Release, March 3, 1993.

28. Jeffrey Denny, "Democrats Play the Soft Money Game," *Common Cause Magazine* 18 (Winter 1992), p. 9.

29. Elizabeth Neuffer, "New Interest Groups Emerge as Big Donors," *Boston Globe*, September 17, 1992, p. 15.

30. Cobb et al., "All the President's Donors," pp. 21–27.

31. Ibid., p. 22.

32. Jeffrey Denny et al., "Bush's Ruling Class," *Common Cause Magazine* 18 (April/May/June 1992), pp. 8–27.

33. See the listing of Team 100 members in Cobb et al., "All the President's Donors."

34. Charles R. Babcock, "GOP Donors Open Wallets For Democrats," *Washington Post*, October 24, 1992, p. A10.

35. Cited in Jill Abramson, "Crowd of Usually Stalwart Pro-GOP Industries Stopped Feeding Elephant as Clinton Surged," *Wall Street Journal*, November 19, 1992, p. A16.

36. See, for example, Alexander, *"Soft Money" and Campaign Financing*; Alexander and Bauer, *Financing the 1988 Election*, pp. 74–82; and Center for Responsive Politics, *Soft Money '88* (Washington, D.C.: Center for Responsive Politics, 1989).

37. FEC, "Democrats Narrow Financial Gap in 1991–92," Press Release, March 11, 1993, pp. 5–6.

38. Michael K. Frisby, "A Spending Problem for the GOP," *Boston Globe*, November 2, 1992, p. 10.

39. Stephen Labaton, "Despite Economy, Clinton Sets Record for Funds," *New York Times*, October 24, 1992, p. 8.

40. Ibid.

41. Frisby, "A Spending Problem for GOP."

42. The three states that did not receive nonfederal funds were Massachusetts, Oklahoma, and West Virginia. These states did receive close to $350,000 in hard money.

43. The eight states that did not receive nonfederal funds were Connecticut, Hawaii, Maryland, Massachusetts, Nebraska, New York, Utah, and West Virginia. Of these, Utah did receive some hard money, but the amount was only $494.

44. The Democratic National Committee conducted polls in Arizona, Nevada, and Virginia in early September but financed no subsequent surveys in these states. The committee also financed one poll in Florida in early October. This was probably due to the fact that the surveys indicated that the Democrats were unlikely to win these states. The only one of these states the Democrats carried in the presidential race was Nevada. In his remarks delivered at the National Press Club on January 19, 1993, James Carville, Clinton's campaign manager, cited Nevada as the one state the Democrats won but had not expected to win.

45. See, for example, the comments by Ellen Miller cited in Labaton, "Despite

Economy, Clinton Sets Record for Funds," and those by Joshua Goldstein cited in Labaton, "Where the 'Soft Money' Comes From," *New York Times*, July 10, 1992, p. A18.

46. Frank J. Sorauf and Scott A. Wilson, "Campaigns and Money: A Changing Role for the Political Parties?" in *The Parties Respond*, ed. by L. Sandy Maisel (Boulder, Colo: Westview Press, 1990), p. 199.

47. Ibid., p. 198.

CHAPTER FOUR

1. Interview with Tad Devine, Manager of Bentsen's Vice-Presidential Campaign, June 29, 1993.

2. Thomas Josefiak, "The '92 Race: Stopping the Buck Here," *Washington Post*, March 10, 1991.

3. Ibid.

4. Herbert E. Alexander, *Reform and Reality* (New York: Twentieth Century Fund Press, 1991), p. 60.

5. See U. S. Senate, *Financing Political Campaigns*, Hearings before the Committee on Finance, 89th Cong., 2nd Sess., August 18 and 19, 1966.

6. Robert Croft, "New York City's Campaign Finance Law—Will It Work?" *The Citizens Budget Commission Quarterly* 8 (Fall 1988), p. 6.

7. FEC, *Annual Report 1990*, p. 40.

8. Ibid.

9. See, among others, Michael Robinson, Clyde Wilcox, and Paul Marshall, "The Presidency: Not for Sale," *Public Opinion* 11 (March/April 1989), pp. 49–53, and David C. Nice, "Campaign Spending and Presidential Election Results," *Polity* 19 (Spring 1987), pp. 464–476.

10. Herbert E. Alexander and Monica Bauer, *Financing the 1988 Election* (Boulder, Colo.: Westview Press, 1991), pp. 138–39.

11. Herbert E. Alexander and Brian A. Haggerty, *Financing the 1984 Election* (Lexington, Mass.: Lexington Books, 1987), p. 271.

12. This proposal was released in a briefing paper by the Executive Office of the President on May 7, 1993. For a discussion, see Richard L. Berke, "Clinton Unveils Plan to Restrict PAC Influence," *New York Times*, May 8, 1993.

13. Center for Responsive Politics, *Soft Money—A Loophole for the '80s* (Washington, D.C.: Center for Responsive Politics, 1985), p. 24.

14. Council on Governmental Ethics Law, *A Model Law for Campaign Finance, Ethics and Lobbying Regulation* (Lexington, Ky., 1990).

15. U.S. Senate Committee on Rules and Administration, *Congressional Spending Limit and Election Reform Act of 1993*, Senate Report 103–41, 103d Cong., 1st sess., April 28, 1993, p. 30.

16. Ibid., p. 29.

INDEX

ABOUT THE AUTHOR

A nthony Corrado is an Assistant Professor of Government at Colby College in Waterville, Maine. He has had extensive practical experience in the management and financing of presidential campaigns as a member of the national staffs of the last three Democratic presidential nominees. In 1992 he served as national campaign coordinator of the Kerrey for President Committee and as a consultant for delegate and convention operations for the Clinton for President Committee. He is the author of *Creative Campaigning: PACs and the Presidential Selection Process* (Westview Press, 1992), as well as a number of articles on presidential campaign finance and the Federal Election Campaign Act.